Sharon Osbourne was born in London in 1952. She is married to rock legend Ozzy Osbourne and has three children: Aimee, Kelly and Jack. She divides her time between Los Angeles and Buckinghamshire

Sharon Osbourne

UNBREAKABLE

SPHERE

First published in Great Britain in 2013 by Sphere
This paperback edition published in 2014 by Sphere

Copyright © Sharon Osbourne 2013

The moral right of the author has been asserted.

All rights reserved.
No part of this publication may be reproduced, stored in a
retrieval system, or transmitted, in any form, or by any means, without
the prior permission in writing of the publisher, nor be otherwise circulated
in any form of binding or cover other than that in which it is published
and without a similar condition including this condition
being imposed on the subsequent purchaser.

A CIP catalogue record for this book
is available from the British Library.

ISBN 978-0-7515-4294-3

Typeset in Bembo by M Rules
Printed and bound in Great Britain by
Clays Ltd, St Ives plc

Papers used by Sphere are from well-managed forests
and other responsible sources.

MIX
Paper from
responsible sources
FSC
www.fsc.org   FSC® C104740

Sphere
An imprint of
Little, Brown Book Group
100 Victoria Embankment
London EC4Y 0DY

An Hachette UK Company
www.hachette.co.uk

www.littlebrown.co.uk

The title of this book is *Unbreakable* and Ozzy, you and I are.

Contents

Prologue

Pearl: a precious jewel whose luminous sheen lights up everything around it. Nature's way of dealing with an imperfection – a piece of grit – in an oyster.

It's said that pearls benefit from being worn as regularly as possible, their lustre improving as they take on the warmth of the skin. I've had pearl earrings and necklaces by the dozen in my time – presents from my father, from my husband, some I've bought myself – but the most precious arrived courtesy of my son. The most valuable pearls, it seems, occur spontaneously in the wild: there is nothing planned or premeditated about them. And the Pearl that came into our lives in April

2012 did exactly that, and she was more precious than anything that emerged from the sea. At first sight of her incandescent beauty my heart soared. All the pain, deception and betrayals of the past few years seemed to evaporate in a single glance from those tiny eyes, those quizzical eyebrows.

Over the last sixty years I have fulfilled various family roles – daughter, sister, wife, mother – all of which, to a greater or lesser extent, I've managed to fuck up. But this is different. The role of grandmother is one that involves no stress, no compromise and no rehearsal. Loving this little scrap of humanity is as natural to me as breathing. I don't think about it, but I can't live without it. At a time in my life when I felt I no longer knew what I was here for, what my role was, this precious Pearl gave me new hope.

While Jackie Boy and his wife Lisa are talking with Ozzy, I sneak into their daughter's bedroom – the one I've made for her in our new house in LA – and stand there mesmerised, gazing down at her tiny body encased in a baby grow, one small hand flung out towards a bar of the cot, miniature fingers curled around it. She stirs slightly, her eyelids flutter and I hold my breath, anxious not to wake her by my presence. But she simply lets out a contented sigh and drifts back to sleep.

Leaning over the cot to kiss her goodnight, my head spins, my senses overwhelmed at the perfection of her tiny ears, as intricate as shells, at each tiny nail, the curve of her neck, and above all, her soft, downy head, cheeks flushed from her goodnight bottle, and that indefinable baby smell of talcum powder that takes me back to my own days as a new mother.

I sit down quietly in the adjacent armchair and glance around the room. It was the first one I had decorated in the new house and it is predominantly pink – what else? No crucifixes and no rubber bats in here . . . Instead, there's a fresco of butterflies painted on the wall above the cot, and framed photographs of dancing ladies in flamboyant gowns. This room, and this little girl dreaming quietly in her cot, represent innocence to me, a brand-new start for all of us.

It's the strangest feeling, becoming a grandmother. You love them as if they're your own but now you have the time to play with them, just to have fun. And you have the wisdom of experience – all those hard lessons you learn over the years as a mother.

Pearl's arrival in our lives has reminded me of all the good times I shared with Aimee, Jack and Kelly. There was a lot of fun – a lot of laughter. But I've also found myself reflecting more upon my mistakes as well. Looking back, it's hardly surprising that motherhood didn't come easily to me. My role models were not only negative, they were positively destructive. A mother who couldn't be arsed to get out of bed to give us breakfast; a father who lied and cheated all his life and for whom I was a useful fall guy – whose word had no more substance to it than a drug addict's promise. Only Sally, my paternal grandmother, could have shown what it meant to be a good parent, but she died before any of the children were born. And then there was Rachel, our housekeeper in LA during the years I got to know Ozzy, a truly wonderful woman who – for as long as I was lucky enough to know her – acted as a surrogate mother to me. And then she was killed in a stupid accident, as unnecessary as it was tragic, a plane crash that also killed Ozzy's best friend and business partner, Randy Rhoads. After that, I buried myself in my work – in Ozzy's career – just keeping the show on the road and, once Aimee,

Kelly and Jack came along, keeping the Osbourne family in funds.

As a mother, I failed. This isn't a statement soliciting a pantomime response, *Oh no you didn't!* I did. The kids said it themselves the first time we all went to a family session when Ozzy was in rehab for the nth time. 'Our father was a drunk and our mother wasn't there for us.' When I look at cine films and later video footage of Aimee, Kelly and Jack when they were young, they bring me a lot of happiness, but they also make me sad because I want to turn back the clock. I want them the way they were then so I can do it all again, now that we've all learnt by our mistakes. Things we should have done, things we *could* have done, but didn't.

Somewhere within that perfect little person are traces of all of us, the good and the bad. I hope at least that Pearl will inherit the long legs and the beauty of her mother. That she'll inherit Jack's happy nature and intelligence. From Lisa's family I hope she has the security of a close-knit community – they all live within a few short miles of each other in Louisiana, and Lisa's parents, and her three sisters, are all happily married. From my father's family, the capacity for survival that brought my grandparents from the ghettos of Eastern Europe. And from my mother's side, the musicality of generations of dancers and entertainers.

And from me? That's a hard one. Not my legs, not my body, for sure. Perhaps my refusal to give up. My unbreakability. But not, I hope, the tendency to take everyone else's problems on my shoulders. To work myself into the ground for all the wrong reasons.

I'm sixty now, and the last decade of my life has been more like the manic schedule of an athletic twenty-three-year-old than a fiftysomething who has survived cancer and years of struggle. It began with *The Osbournes* TV show. I'd always been happy working as Ozzy's manager, hiding in the background. Now I was thrust into the limelight. And after a failed talk show in the US, Simon Cowell offered me a judging role on *The X Factor*. Suddenly – and quite unexpectedly – I had begun a career in television. I was proud of that – I liked the fact that this was *my* work. And for the first time in my career I was actually doing something for me, something that I loved doing. Remember I was a failed drama school kid who was never good enough to get work as an actress or dancer. Finally, my time as the main 'talent' (whatever the fuck that means) had come, later in life.

The trouble was, I could never reach the point where I could sit back and say, 'Enough. You've proved you can do it, now sit back. Relax. Just enjoy life.' I just couldn't stop – jumping on and off planes, taking on more and more work and weeping with exhaustion as I made late-night calls to my family on the other side of the world.

I convinced myself that my kids were all grown up and independent – that they didn't really need me any more. So however much they begged me to stop – not for *their* benefit, but for my own health – I carried on with the same crazy schedule, burning myself out in the process. There was always a small voice whispering in the back of my mind – that if I just worked a bit harder, carried on for a little bit longer, I would somehow be a better person. That people would value me and love me more. That I would respect *myself* more. And so it went on, year after year.

Until now. As I sit here, the rhythmic ebb and flow of my granddaughter's breathing calms me like nothing else, and I know that *she* will prove to be my line in the sand. I have survived colon cancer and had a double mastectomy to thwart potential breast cancer, my precious son has been diagnosed with a life-threatening illness and here, right in front of me, is his brand-new little daughter with all the vulnerability, promise and hope she brings. How many more signs do I need before I accept that it's time to stand still, take stock and appreciate what I have in front of me rather than haring around the world, ceaselessly chasing some mythical ideal of what *I* misguidedly think is the 'perfect' life?

My defining moment came in June this year, 2013, in the early hours of the morning in a hotel somewhere in the UK. I woke up with a start, my heart thumping, my neck clammy with sweat, and I genuinely hadn't the faintest clue where I was. I lay there for what felt like hours, but was probably just a few seconds, scrabbling for clues. Had I been on a plane? If so, where had I flown in from? Was I filming in this unknown place? If so, which show? Where was Ozzy? Where were the kids? Were any of the dogs with me? Eventually, by retracing the conversations and events of the past few days, I worked out that I was in Birmingham for the audition stages of this year's *X Factor*.

I peered at the bedside clock: 3 a.m. That meant 7 p.m. LA time, just as my gorgeous 'Pearly girl', as I like to call her, would be going to bed. Firing my laptop into life, I clicked on Facetime and dialled Jack.

'It's Nana,' I croaked, my voice suffering as it always does when I'm run down. 'Can I speak to my scrumptious granddaughter, please?'

And suddenly, there she was, blinking incomprehensibly at the screen, wondering why she could see Nana but not touch her. She'd just had a bath and her wisps of hair were damp, slicked to one side. The urge to reach into the screen and hug her overwhelmed me. I felt the familiar prick of impending tears. What was I doing, sitting in a hotel room thousands of miles away from my family, when real life, in all its Technicolor, unpredictable glory, was going on at home? What was I trying to prove?

I loved doing *The X Factor* when it started in 2004 and, after leaving under a cloud in 2007, I was thrilled when they asked me to return for the current, tenth-anniversary series. For me, it was a chance to complete the circle. But after much thought, I've decided it will be the last one I ever do. Don't get me wrong – when I'm there, in the moment, I love every minute. And I don't want to stop working completely. But I do want to slow down.

More than anything, I want to play with my grand-daughter, right here in this beautiful house that I hope will be the heart of our family life, the perfect meeting place for all our children, *their* children, dogs, friends, whenever they're in town. And with Pearly girl as my guiding light, I think I'm getting there.

She lets out a small sigh and turns over again, her breathing shallower now. In a few seconds, she will wake up and we'll have playtime together. I gently stroke her hair and she opens her hazel eyes, blinking in the half-light, uncertain for a moment of where she is. I know that feeling.

'It's Nana, my darling girl.' I lift her out of the cot and press her soft, warm body to mine. 'Shall we go and find the doggies?'

I take her through to the kitchen where my faithful Pomeranian, Bella, is waiting for us. Using my free hand, I scoop her up and she nestles in the crook of my arm, purring with pleasure. With her short, soft fur, her diminutive size and her fondness for doing fuck-all squared, she's a cat by any other name.

'Come on, my darlings,' I say softly, heading out towards a shaded corner of the garden. 'Let's see what the day brings us, shall we?'

1

The Exit Factor

My final series of *The X Factor* did have a few fun moments.

On 20 October 2007, I stepped out on to the *X Factor* stage for the first live show of the fourth series. For three great years I'd had so much fun, helped some really talented people get their first break, thrown a few gallons of water over Louis Walsh and had a spat or three with Simon Cowell. I hadn't laughed so much in a job in my life, or felt more comfortable.

I had spent a lifetime riding a roller-coaster, barely clinging on with my fingernails, from my chaotic childhood and confused adolescence to the adrenalin-fuelled years of life on the road, managing my husband's career. Finally things seemed to be slowing down. I'd beaten cancer. My children were all doing well. Ozzy and I had moved into our new home a long way from the mad-house that became familiar to millions of viewers in *The Osbournes*, and we were looking forward to spending more time together and considering the possibility that we might even grow old.

The summer of 2007 had been a watershed. At the end of July, I lost my father. Don Arden was a legend in the industry, the Al Capone of rock promoters, famed and feared from LA to London. We'd spent half our lives at loggerheads – for twenty years we didn't even speak – but he was still my dad, a man I looked up to, who taught me all I knew and whom, for all his many, many faults, I loved. For the past few years he had been suffering from Alzheimer's, and the control freak who would happily have seen me dead a decade earlier was replaced by a sad old man who didn't know where or who he was, let alone anyone else. To be honest, his death came as a relief – at the end, he was just an empty shell and life held no more enjoyment for him. At least now the suffering was over.

That evening at Wembley should have felt like a homecoming, but as the audience roared us to our seats at the judges' table, I had a tight knot like a fist in my stomach. I knew before the show got started that this year was going to be very different. In fact, that's an understatement. It would prove to be a nightmare.

Looking back now, the signs were there from the start. I was just too busy and too tired to spot them. The success of a show like *The X Factor* depends not only on the quality of the contestants, but also on the chemistry that exists between the judges. And for some reason, the mix of Simon, Louis and myself had worked. We sparked off each other; there was a healthy rivalry, and we each brought something subtly different to the mix. Simon had strength of character and he was opinionated and outspoken. I was also very direct but delivered the message with more heart. In addition, Simon and I never agreed about anything, which made for good television. As for Louis, not only does he have a great knowledge of music and the business, he also has a fantastic sense of humour and he loved to egg us on. He was the one with the spoon stirring it all up. We weren't in competition with each other, not outside of the terms of the format of the show.

The first I knew that something was up was when I

had a call from the producer, Richard Holloway, who told me that Louis had been fired. I was shocked.

Simon is someone who can't stand still; he likes change. And as the owner and executive producer of the show, he could do whatever he liked. It was his prerogative. But I never for one minute thought it would happen. There was no personal animosity between them – on the contrary. Simon had signed two of Louis's biggest bands so they had ongoing business together.

We soon learnt that getting shot of Louis wasn't the last of the changes Simon had in mind. A fourth judge would be joining us, Dannii Minogue. I knew nothing about Dannii beyond her being Kylie's sister, and I have always had a great respect for Kylie. But in one of those strange coincidences it turned out that my then PA, Silvana, who herself hailed from Down Under, actually knew Dannii personally. Silvana's sister Tina, also a singer, had been at school with her, and in fact she and Dannii had started off in TV together. 'You'll love her,' Silvana said. And I had no reason not to believe her.

So on day one, there were four of us. Simon and me,

then Dannii and Brian Friedman, an American choreographer drafted in to replace Louis. On day two Simon took me to one side.

'It's not working, is it?'

'No, it's not,' I said. 'It's terrible.'

'I'll get rid of Brian,' he said.

'Bring back Louis while you're at it.'

And so it came to pass.

If I'm honest, I'd expected Dannii to be a bit flossy and sweet. She looked like a little doll! But I quickly realised she was sharp, smart and ambitious. I respected that and thought she could bring something new to the show.

And that was about the extent of my thoughts on Dannii during the early audition stages. She had seemed fine at that point. But then again, I hadn't really had much to do with her. The audition stages can be quite a slog, travelling up and down the country. On top of that, I was making the journey over from LA. It was Birmingham one week, Manchester the next, Glasgow another, Cardiff another . . . So by the time I'd finished a long day of filming and given it my va-va-voom all, I'd invariably just retire to my room, have a bath, snuggle up in my favourite pink, fluffy dressing gown that goes everywhere with me, then call Ozzy and the kids to see how their day had been.

More often than not, my body clock was still on LA time anyway, so hanging around the hotel bar after filming had never been my thing. I might have managed it once or twice, but most nights I could be happily curled up in bed by 9 p.m. So at this stage, I had only really seen Dannii when we were filming, we didn't socialise. From what I could tell, she seemed needy on set, but not with me. As it was her first time on the show, I think she was just keen to get it right, which was fair enough. As I say, she never bothered me. I would just do my bit then go off and seek my own space which, believe me, when you've had cameras thrust in your face all day, you desperately need.

After the audition stage had finished, I headed off back to America for the rest of the summer. The plan was to squirrel away at home and stay below the media parapet until the live shows started in October, so I didn't do any interviews during this period and, being in the US, I wasn't seeing any British newspapers at all.

However, my publicist in England would send me

anything that related to me, and things started appearing in the press about how I was jealous of Dannii because I'm so much older, she's so young and pretty, she's so talented, she's so this, she's so that . . . blah, blah, the usual bollocks. I have been in the business a long time and know only too well that the media loves a good old feud story, it's all part of the game. If you prod someone in the chest with a finger it gets blown out of all proportion and becomes a 'punch-up', but at least the story usually has *some* tiny germ of truth in it. However, this one didn't and I genuinely had no problem with Dannii at all.

At first, I just mentally swatted it away, like an irritating fly. Tomorrow, I told myself, it will be chip paper. But the same theme kept on reappearing, building up a head of steam. As I hadn't done any interviews about *The X Factor*, I couldn't put the record straight. But never once in any interview that I'd read – and she seemed to have done about a million of the bloody things, and front-cover stories too – had Dannii said something along the lines of, 'Look, that's ridiculous, we get on just fine and there's absolutely no problem here.' And it irritated the hell out of me, because it was very simple: deny it and kill the myth. So I'm not saying she perpetuated it, but from what I read she certainly didn't deflect it either.

By the time the first live show came around, I had worked myself up into a bit of a lather, particularly as the same old shit about me being jealous had started up *again*. Once you're on set, you hit the ground running. There's barely time to run to the loo during rehearsals, let alone address a thorny issue, so I decided that backstage before the live show started would be the best option.

Silvana and I talked tactics and decided that, given her history and friendship with Dannii, it would be friendlier and less confrontational if she approached her on my behalf.

So she headed off down the corridor, popped her head round Dannii's dressing-room door and asked politely whether she had a couple of minutes spare to have a quick chat with me.

No, she couldn't come now as she was getting ready, and apparently up against the clock. Well, that pissed me off. We had at least another two hours before the show started, so we were hardly pushed for time. Given the circumstances, I thought she could have been more gracious.

About half an hour later, I asked Silvana if she would mind returning to the little madam's boudoir and asking again whether she could spare some of her precious time to grant me a brief audience. She reappeared again a couple of minutes later, looking sheepish.

'Sorry, it's another no. Maybe later.'

That was it. I felt the familiar hot swell of fury rise in my chest, the same red mist that has blurred my better judgement on countless other occasions. I admit it. I have a very bad temper, but at times like this I just can't help it. I'm someone who wears my heart on my sleeve and I can't be contrived. Much as I would sometimes like to, I can't have a stern word with myself and retreat into a corner until I'm more composed. After an outburst, I have often reflected that it would have been far better to retaliate with a measured, devastatingly damning riposte. But instead, I always go BANG, say what's on my mind and then think, Oh shit, did I *really* just do that?

So I was off, heading out of the door like an Exocet missile propelled by sheer fury.

As well as Silvana, my publicist Gary Farrow was in my dressing room at the time, and so was the woman in charge of press for Simon Cowell's TV company Syco.

'You lot are coming with me because I am going in that fucking dressing room *now*.' I just wanted to deal with it.

I went charging down the hallway and hammered on the door. When her shocked assistant answered, I threw myself into the room. Dannii was sitting in front of the mirror, being made up. She had rollers in her hair, but still looked annoyingly gorgeous.

'I want a word with you. What the *fuck* is going on?' I demanded.

'What are you talking about? I don't understand.' Her mouth had fallen open in shock.

'I have absolutely no problem with you, so what's all this negative press?'

'I honestly don't know what you are talking about. This is ridiculous.' She looked uncomfortable. 'I've got to get ready and I'm nervous, this is my first live show . . .'

And that was it. She turned back to the mirror and made it very clear that the conversation, if that's what you could call it, was over.

Nervous! Oh *please*, she'd been prancing up and down on stages since she was a fucking foetus, so the notion that a few TV cameras were suddenly going to faze her was utterly laughable. Gary could sense that I still had plenty of fuel left in my tank for carrying it on, so got hold of my arm and started to guide me towards the exit.

'Just stop it,' I shot back over my shoulder at Dannii before flouncing out with as much dignity as I could muster.

It was her birthday that day and what made it even more annoying was that I had bought her a gorgeous Chanel handbag, which I'd left in her room earlier with a little card. It had cost me eighteen hundred quid; a lot of money whichever way you look at it. Oh well, I thought, she'll probably give back the handbag after my little outburst, so at least something good will come of it. I rather fancied it for myself anyway. But no. Just as Zsa Zsa Gabor once said that she never hated a man enough to give back his diamonds, Dannii Minogue clearly didn't hate me enough to give back a designer handbag.

A little later, we were all standing behind the giant screen that the judges walk through at the start of each live show. Simon was on camera right, with Dannii next to him, then me, then Louis. Me and Louis were in a heightened state of anticipation, sharing jokes. By then, I had virtually forgotten the little contretemps. I had made my position clear – albeit loudly and colourfully – and, as far as I was concerned, we could move on.

But to my left? *Nada*. It was like the Berlin Wall had been rebuilt in the six-inch space between us. She wouldn't even look at me. You could have cut the atmosphere with a knife. She started whispering something in Simon's ear, like a bloody kid in the playground, and Louis rolled his eyes at me. We felt like we had herpes.

Then suddenly *The X Factor* theme tune came powering out of the speakers, once again sending goosebumps up my arms and back. I could feel the adrenalin pumping around my body, prompting a delicious exhilaration that, just for a few seconds, always made me feel invincible. And, invariably, prompted me to do something mischievous.

As the screen opened and we walked out to the thundering roar of the audience, I reached across and grabbed Dannii's hand, yanking it up into the air in a triumphant punch. Much later, in her autobiography, she writes about this moment as if it was something she welcomed, a peace offering that made her feel all warm and gooey inside, as if everything might turn out OK between us. Utter bilge, if you ask me. I could feel she was fighting with all her teensy weensy might to put her arm down and extricate herself from my grip, but as she only weighs about 3lb, I successfully managed to keep her arm up there, grinning maniacally and thinking, Fuck *you*, missus.

Dannii is stunning to look at, even prettier than Kylie, actually. Her skin is incredible and she has a perfectly proportioned figure, thanks to a little help on the top half. And of course, Simon fancied the pants off her. I get that. He's single, he's the boss and he can do what the fuck he wants.

But during filming it was obvious to me that there was some sort of relationship going on between them and, the more it progressed, the worse it became between her and me. It was unbelievably bad. She had now taken to walking past me in the hallway without even making eye contact. I'd like to say it didn't bother me, but it did. A lot. After all, who wants to work in such an unpleasant atmosphere? The days were long and hard enough without the extra burden of spending hours sitting next to someone with a face like a smacked arse.

I had really enjoyed the previous three series, but this one was rapidly turning into an odious chore. I found it hard dealing with a sulker. So after a couple of weeks of this icy nonsense, I decided to instigate a meeting with her and executive producer Richard Holloway. I wanted to bury the hatchet. You can ignore an unpleasant frisson if it's just for one day, but this was going on and on, doing my head in.

The meeting was held in an empty dressing room at Wembley, on a Friday when we were doing rehearsals with our acts for the next night's live show. It was just the three of us and she perched on top of the counter along one wall, her legs dangling, her eyes staring straight ahead as if she was transfixed by something on the opposite side of the room. Anything but look at Richard and me who were sitting adjacent to her on a sofa. I cleared my throat and aimed my words at the side of her head.

'Look, I apologise if I have offended you. This isn't pleasant for either of us; I just want to clear things up so we can get a more harmonious atmosphere.'

Nothing. Her gaze didn't shift from the far wall, so I carried on.

'What is it you want from me so we can get this to a professional level and get it to work? Shall I walk over hot coals? Eat broken glass?'

Again, nothing. Not. One. Fucking. Word.

Richard started talking to her in a low voice and she mumbled back at him, then he declared that as we didn't seem to be getting anywhere we might as well draw the meeting to a close. And that was it. My attempt at making peace had fallen on deaf ears and we were back to cold shoulders and frosty silences. It was all far too school playground for me.

Thank God I had asked Richard to be there, because if you repeat these things, people might say you're exaggerating, that she must have said *something*. But no, she said fuck all to me. Outwardly, she seemed all 'Ooh, I *love* children, I *love* puppies', but in my opinion she was dark, very dark. What you saw was most definitely not what you got.

And so the show went on, and on, and bloody on, for what, given the unpleasantness, seemed like an age to me. The closer she got to Simon, the more I felt that she started telling the producers what to do. Suddenly, from being the supposedly nervous new girl, she was saying, 'This isn't right,' and, 'Simon doesn't like it this way.'

Every time I heard her do it, I had to embed my teeth in the end of my tongue to stop myself making a caustic remark. I'm surprised there's not a dent in it to this day. Meanwhile, the antics behind the screen had gone up a gear, with her sticking her tongue in Simon's ear and giggling like a bloody teenager whilst Louis and me stood there like a couple of gooseberries.

Then again, Simon was single and so was she. They could do what they wanted. But, for me, it made her *so* unbearable to work with that I just couldn't take it. It was horrible. My stomach was constantly knotted with anxiety about it and as each show loomed I would wake up and think, Oh God, I have to spend the day sitting alongside *her* again. It had become intolerable so I asked to have a meeting with Simon.

He was staying in a suite at the Mandarin Oriental hotel in central London and liked to hold any meetings there, so he slotted me in for later that day. It was towards the end of filming *The X Factor* live shows, so the final was imminent and this series was about to become just a bad memory. I was here to fight my corner for the next one. I walked in, gave him a kiss on each cheek and launched straight in.

'I can't take it any more. It's her or me.'

His expression remained impassive. Simon is used to dealing with various ongoing spats between the women in his life and clearly takes it all in his stride.

'I'm not going to make that choice, Sharon. I would like both of you to stay.'

Inwardly, my heart sank. This was not what I wanted to hear, so I acted like he hadn't said it and persevered.

'Look, if you did some audience research, I don't think she's even got a particularly strong fan base.'

'What do you mean?' He sounded weary.

'She had a single out in the middle of the series, and it tanked.'

He stuck his bottom lip out, then shrugged.

'It doesn't matter. When I was on *American Idol* with Paula Abdul, she released a single that didn't do very well either. But the audience still loved her.'

I could sense that the battle was lost, but I was a desperate woman so had one last try.

'Dannii's just a pretty face. You can get another pretty face.'

'Sharon, I'm not doing it.' His firm tone left me in no doubt that this wasn't a matter for debate. 'I don't want you to go and I don't want her to go either. So think about it.'

We were about to finish the series and then it was Christmas. Simon clearly thought that I would fly back to LA, spend some downtime with Ozzy and the kids, then calm down and change my mind about leaving the show.

In a way, he was right. Christmas came and went, and there was so much else going on, not least being a judge on the next series of *America's Got Talent*. *The X Factor* wasn't a topic of conversation at home; I think everyone in the family just presumed that I would go back. By the time March 2008 came around, the memory of all the angst had dulled slightly, so I *did* start negotiations for the next series, pencilling it into my schedule for that summer.

I'm first and foremost a businesswoman, so, knowing

that I was quite in demand at the time, I decided to try and up my deal a bit. Men always get more money, that's just the way it is, and I thought, Fuck it, I'm going to push, push, push. With stuff like that, it's OK. I'm not asking Mrs Smith next door to bust her balls, I'm dealing with a corporation. The game is that you go in, ask for too much and know you're not going to get it, then settle for something in the middle.

Negotiations started and we were going back and forth on the money, unable to agree. On top of that, about a month before the auditions were set to start, I felt the familiar churning sensation in my gut at the thought of going through all that old shit again. There I was, in my lovely home, enjoying a relatively peaceful life with my family, about to leave them for a manic schedule of different cities and hotels alongside someone I was uncomfortable with, someone who gave me a fucking great knot in my stomach. What was I doing? It wasn't that I was afraid, more anxious. I started weighing up the pros and cons in my mind constantly, the only pro being the money. I went over it with Ozzy so many times that I think he stopped listening.

'I don't think I'm going to go back.'

'Sharon, do what you've got to do, it's your call. I just don't want it making you ill.'

He had a point. I don't handle that kind of stress at all well; it eats me up. It was just the thought of that toxic atmosphere again; of standing behind that screen just inches away from someone exuding utter disdain. I wasn't building a career, I wasn't promoting a record, I wasn't hoping to get signed by a label. So why do it? It was like a spider's web for me. There had been no humour, no fun moments, and I just didn't want the pressure again.

Ultimately, the reason I didn't do the next series was because I didn't get the money I wanted, but the Dannii business was all mixed in there too. Afterwards, I spoke to Simon on the phone and he was really nice about it. I was still working for him on *America's Got Talent*, so I knew that we were absolutely fine going forward. That's one of the really good things about Simon: you can say your piece and he never holds it against you.

In fact, it was Louis and me who came up with the idea that he should replace me with Cheryl Cole. A decision that, ultimately, worked out really well for everyone.

*

When the publicity started for the next series with Cheryl Cole instead of me, word reached me back in LA that the stock line seemed to be that I had kicked up a stink because I felt threatened by the presence of another woman on the panel.

As I now work with four other women on a daily talk show in LA and get on famously with every single one of them, it's quite clear to me that when people clash, it has absolutely nothing to do with gender and everything to do with their personality differences.

We get on really well now, but when I had a bit of a ding-dong with Piers Morgan during the second season of *America's Got Talent*, no one suggested that it had anything to do with what sex we were. It was just a plain old clash of characters, that's it. There I was, a successful businesswoman in my fifties, a mother, a wife, and already well established as a judge on the show, being made out to be jealous of a young, single woman who, as far as I am concerned, can't sing for shit and couldn't cut a business deal if she fucking tried. Give me a break.

When the book *Sweet Revenge: The Intimate Life Of Simon Cowell* came out in April 2012, the author Tom

Bower wrote that Simon had said the following about Dannii: 'I had a crush on her. It was Dannii's hair, the sexy clothes and the tits. I was like a schoolboy. She was foxy. She was a real man's girl. Very feminine.' Bower also wrote that Simon had told a friend, 'There were a few bonks and then it petered out while I was in America.'

Publicly, Simon still hasn't admitted to the affair, but Bower told the media that he had confirmed it to him privately. When I heard this, I felt like shouting from the rooftops, '*See*? I was right.'

I wouldn't say I felt vindicated as such, because I didn't feel guilty of anything in the first place, but it proved I hadn't been making it up when I said she had an uppity attitude as she was fucking the boss. To my mind, she must have felt it was a case of 'Don't fuck with me, because I'll tell him'. She clearly felt that shagging Simon gave her a vicarious power and it was so immature, not to mention deeply bloody irritating to deal with. Now that she's in her forties and has a young child, she's probably a very different person. The trouble is, when you get by on your looks, where do you go as you get older? But to be honest, other than having to remember what happened between us for the purposes of writing this book I just don't think about her now. If I saw her at an event, I wouldn't say anything. I probably wouldn't even acknowledge her.

Now, as I enter my seventh decade, I find I *am* losing my temper less often, probably more to do with wilful self-improvement than any chemical shift prompted by age. I am really trying not to be confrontational, but at least if I am, I find that I can get it out there in a more measured way and then move on.

These days, if someone is doing something I think is annoying or wrong, or I just don't agree with it, then I'll say, look, whatever you're doing is wrong and it's annoying me, so would you please stop. Or words to that effect, give or take the odd cuss here and there. Then they will either deny it, tell me I'm imagining it, or admit it and say that now they know it bothers me they will stop forthwith. Then it's done. No grudges. I'm not the sort of person who will hate you or never talk to you again. I'm just not that way. Besides, things change in a second and you might suddenly see a quality in that person that you've never seen before, something you didn't notice when you first met them. So you can't use a first meeting as a barometer, I know that now. I have definitely become less kneejerk in my reactions to people and, I hope, more tolerant.

When it was announced that I was going to be a judge on the tenth series of *The X Factor* this year, naturally the press, ever keen to stir up a feud, asked Dannii for her thoughts on my return.

'That's risky. Either people will go, "We have moved on," or go, "Amazing." I won't be watching, I haven't watched any of the shows since I left,' she replied.

Obviously, I took the job and I certainly wouldn't have done so if *I* thought it was a risky decision for either me or the show, so I don't agree with her. But you know what? The older, wiser, mellower me feels that nobody agrees on absolutely everything and that she's perfectly entitled to her opinion. It really doesn't bother me.

Knock yourself out, Dannii love.

For me, this whole sorry episode in my life can be summed up by something Ozzy said at the time. Unless someone is a really well-established star, he hardly ever knows who they are, and sometimes I can tell him a story a hundred times and he forgets what I've said. I'm sure that, during the early audition stages, I had told him I was working with Dannii, before it all went horribly wrong. But knowing him, he probably hadn't computed the information.

Anyway, the night of the showdown in her dressing room, I came home to Welders, our home in Buckinghamshire, tired and upset. I was still in turmoil about it, and I curled up on our sofa in the kitchen and let rip with, 'Dannii Minogue did this,' and 'Dannii Minogue did that,' as Ozzy sat opposite me.

After a couple of minutes, I glanced across to find him looking faintly perplexed.

'I didn't know Kylie had a brother.'

2

Minnie

A woman's best friend.

There was another reason why series four of *The X Factor* was such a strain. Ever since I'd started working on the show I'd had a special companion – someone who always took my side, defended me at every turn . . . and could bite your hand off if she felt like it. No human could ever fill this role. I am talking about Minnie, my unutterably gorgeous, white fluffy Pomeranian who was the canine love of my life. She was my best friend in the world and went everywhere with me. But during that last season, she had got a lot quieter and I'd started to worry about her. I wondered if the constant travelling, the interminable transatlantic flights, weren't taking their toll.

Originally she had been Kelly's dog, but from the moment she and I met, we just connected. It was kismet, and she never left my side. Every single day for the previous twelve years she had been there, no matter what. During those terrible months when I had colon cancer, unable and unwilling to communicate with human beings, she was glued to my side, even in the hospital. If I went to make a cup of tea, she would wake up from her snooze and follow me to the kitchen. If I got up to go to the toilet in the middle of the night, there she would be trotting along beside me. When Ozzy and I went on tour, she would just pine and refuse to eat until we got back. In the end we had no option but to take her with us, and she and Maggie – a Japanese Chin that we got at the same time – became a familiar sight on the hard-rock circuit.

Her loyalty and her devotion to me were quite extraordinary. But she didn't see herself as a lapdog. She was my guard dog, albeit a diminutive one, but what she lacked in stature she made up for in ferocity, snapping at anyone who came too close to her precious mama.

The list of those who learnt to give her a wide berth could be enough for a feature in *Hello!* magazine. She went for Piers Morgan backstage at *America's Got Talent*. She had also taken chunks out of Patrick Swayze and David Hasselhoff. Even Ozzy incurred her wrath on a regular basis. Every time he got into bed, she would curl her lip at him and make low growling noises.

'Fucking hell, Sharon, it's been *twelve years*. Surely she must recognise me by now?'

Poms live to a good age – often as old as eighteen – so that April I had no reason to worry when she started to cough. But we knew she had had heart issues for a couple of years, and we'd been told to watch her weight, but I didn't put two and two together.

It was a Saturday evening in July 2008. Ozzy and I were at home, enjoying the comparative peace of our new house at Hidden Hills, a gated community in Calabasas right on the northernmost tip of LA with nothing else beyond it except wilderness. The dogs, of course, loved the space and freedom it gave them. Even Minnie had been known to gambol about on the grass. Not this night. She was curled up beside me, not even moving when I did. Something wasn't right. I was aware that she was unable to walk more than a few yards without needing to rest. And now there was the coughing. I had got used to it over the preceding few months. It was Ozzy who picked up that tonight something was different. Although by now it was gone ten, I called Dr Lisa, the vet who'd looked after all our dogs since way back when and whose practice was in Malibu, where we used to spend our summers and where we bought so many of our dogs. She was usually happy to make house calls, and with sixteen dogs to take care of, from inoculations to minor ailments, she was a regular visitor to Hidden Hills. However, this time she said we should bring Minnie to the clinic immediately. There were scans that would need to be done in situ, she explained. Malibu lies ten or so miles up the coast north of Los Angeles, on the narrow strip of road known as the Pacific Coast Highway which is squeezed in between the Santa Monica Mountains and the ocean. As the crow flies it's not that far from Hidden Hills – roughly due west. But there are mountains in between, and the only way down is through the canyons, on the kind of road they use in advertisements for sports cars, and which only the foolhardy would dream of driving down at night. That's the way we went. Ozzy had only just passed his test so his driving skills were at best unpolished, and when he braked, you knew it. This road demanded near-constant braking as bend followed vertiginous bend. With Minnie cradled on my lap, we set off. Her breathing was rasping and her eyes were watering, the tears falling on my hands as I stroked her soft, pale fur, something I had done so very often. We were there in less than half an hour and by the time we arrived, Lisa had opened up the clinic and called in a heart specialist. We were asked to sit in the waiting room while they ran some tests. Ozzy and I sat there holding hands, saying nothing. When they called us in, Minnie was lying on her side, just panting, unable to move. They had strapped on a little oxygen mask which looked like a child's toy. They needed to do a few more tests, they said. We should go home and phone in an hour when they'd have a clearer picture.

So back we went up that dark, winding road, back to the house, back to the kitchen with all the dogs ranged around us. I put the kettle on and we had a cup of tea. All the time I was watching the clock and the moment the hour was up, I called.

'What did she say?' asked Ozzy when I came off the phone.

'She wants us to go back.'

'What, now?'

'Now. We have to make a decision.'

Dr Lisa didn't embellish it, but we understood. We both knew what that decision was. I was hysterical, but Ozzy stayed calm. He knew what Minnie meant to me. We got back in the car and Ozzy twisted his way down the canyon to Malibu. I was still in my pyjama bottoms, a hooded top and flip-flops.

The moment we arrived I went straight in to Minnie who was lying on her side, still, though she attempted to wave her front paws when I picked her off the cold steel examination table to comfort her.

There was nothing they could do, Lisa said. So we had a choice. She could either come home with us, and we could wait for nature to take its course – a day or two at most. But we had to bear in mind that she was extremely uncomfortable, she explained. The alternative was that they gave her an injection there and then.

I knew I couldn't leave her in discomfort for my own selfish reasons, just for me to have one more day, one more night to hold her, to put my nose in her fur and breathe her in. I just couldn't do it. Ozzy agreed. They put us in a little anteroom and I sat there with her on my knee, her little head resting on the bend of my elbow, her dry nose on my arm. And all the while I was talking to her, reminding her of all we'd been through together, telling her how much I loved her. Her eyes, which had been wide open when we first brought her in, were now half closed though the tears were still flowing, leaving matted stains on her face. Lisa gave her a shot of Valium first, to allow her to go to sleep normally before the final injection. That was the plan, anyway. But she was so weak that the Valium proved to be enough. Within seconds her breathing got shallower and shallower and then it stopped. She died in my arms.

Emotionally distraught as I was, there were the inevitable practicalities to attend to.

Lisa explained that we could either bury her at home, or she could be cremated. They'd send her body away and her remains would be returned to us by mail. *By mail?* I mean, how would you know whose ashes you were getting? It struck me as so cold and undignified. Minnie deserved better than being posted off somewhere. The decision was made: we would take her home. That night, back at Hidden Hills, I put her in her basket – a child's toy in the shape of a lamb, lined with soft fleece – wrapped in one of my shawls. She'd always had a thing about Ozzy's socks, piling them up on our bed, so I found an old pair and tucked them under her. The air-conditioning in the downstairs cloakroom wasn't working properly, so it was always freezing in there, and that's where we put her. She looked so peaceful – there was nothing to show that she wasn't just sleeping, so I took some pictures and cut off some of her beautiful fur as a memento.

It happened that we had carpenters working in the house, so the next morning Ozzy asked them to build Minnie a little coffin made of oak, a wood that would last, he said. Then, with all due ceremony, we buried her under a willow tree in the garden. To mark the place, I had her name carved on a rock beneath the sign of an angel.

I realise that some people will find it hard to understand how I could be so affected by the death of a dog. But throughout my life I have been betrayed, by my mother, by my father, by my first boyfriend and by my husband. Minnie never betrayed me, and I loved her for that.

Maggie, her constant companion, spent the next

weeks looking for her. It was heartbreaking; she would search constantly, going into room after room. Her tail, usually like a quivering question mark, began to droop, and it stayed that way until she died this year. By that time we had sold Hidden Hills and I knew I couldn't leave Minnie to be dug up by a fox or a bulldozer making way for an outhouse or whatever. Luckily, one of the biggest pet cemeteries in Los Angeles was just down the road, so we disinterred her, drove to the pet cemetery and waited as she was cremated. We chose an urn to put her ashes in, and they're on top of the fireplace in our living room in Beverly Hills. In due course, Maggie joined her. Maggie was sixteen, blind and deaf when she passed in her sleep.

And despite her penchant for biting him, Ozzy loved Minnie too. He was hurting because I was. He's a huge Beatles fan and, when he first met Paul McCartney, he had a photo taken with him. That photo meant so much to him that he had a solid gold picture frame made for it, with musical notes engraved around the side. But after Minnie died, he did the sweetest thing. He took his cherished photo out, replaced it with one of Minnie and gave it to me with a handwritten inscription.

Minnie was bigger than any Beatle.

It turned out that Piers had a soft spot for Minnie too, despite her regular attacks on him. After her death he wrote a tribute to her in the *Mail On Sunday*:

For the last two years, the bane of my life has been Sharon Osbourne's small white Pomeranian dog, Minnie. Every time I went near this ferocious creature, it would go berserk – snarling, growling and attempting to bite me. A behavioural pattern, in fact, rather similar to its owner. Minnie died this week, after a long illness. And I found myself feeling unexpectedly sad. 'I can't believe I'm saying this, but I'll actually miss her,' I told a heartbroken Sharon on the phone tonight. 'She was a real character.' I don't normally 'do' dogs, but this was no ordinary dog.

3

Reloaded

The Osbournes back together again.

After the dramas of *The X Factor* and the loss of my beloved Minnie, I retreated to Hidden Hills. *America's Got Talent* was over for another season, and I planned to enjoy being a wife and mother again. Jack and Aimee were both based in LA and, like any mum, I kept an eye on them while trying my best not to interfere.

Kelly was another matter. She'd been living in London for a couple of years by then. She'd gone back originally in 2007, opening on 10 September for a seven-week run playing Mama Morton in *Chicago*, the youngest actress ever to take the role. I remember going to the opening night and being staggered at what she had achieved. Although one of nature's drama queens, she had never acted professionally and yet here she was, starting at the top, wowing a West End audience and the critics, too. The following June she won the *Glamour* magazine award for Best Theatre Actress. Kelly's vivacious personality was perfect for musical theatre, and London took her to its heart. The prodigal daughter – she was born just down the road, after all – was hired by Radio 1 to host a Sunday-night show, *The Surgery*, where she answered young people's questions. It was an inspired choice, because she had packed a lot into her twenty-three years and her natural rebelliousness resonated with her generation, although from my point of view she'd probably seen too much for her own good. While I took pride in her success, I hated being so far away from her. However much we talked on the phone, I missed our cuddles, and it's hard to pick up those clues that things aren't going well if you're several thousand miles away.

My real worry was drugs. It was common knowledge that, over the years, Kelly had struggled with addiction. She had checked into rehab back in 2004 and then again in 2005, but I remained optimistic that the dark days were behind us. But without being able to look her in the eyes, it was hard to be sure. Still, you never know. She was young, and like all young people she was finding herself, which necessarily involves being influenced by your friends and peer group – the people you hang out with. And I knew who she was hanging out with – the press made sure of that – and I knew that there were at least some among them who did drugs. While I understand that experimentation is all part of growing up, I was worried. I was never an addict – I have never even smoked a cigarette – but her father did, and he was.

Yet like all young people, she wanted to be accepted into this new community, the beautiful people who lived on those renowned London hills. And she was both vulnerable and gullible. Once you are 'famous', friendships are difficult. It takes years of experience to be able to work out just why people are paying you attention. Do they really like you for who you are? Or is there something else at work? When I first moved to LA at around the same age as Kelly, I had power and influence through my father, a huge name in the music industry both in the States and in England. Sharon

Arden could get VIP passes to see Led Zeppelin or the Stones with one phone call. Being on the inside track brought me instant friends. But it came at a cost, both emotional and financial. And I feared for Kelly that the same thing would happen to her. It did, and I could only watch from afar as a succession of nonentities came, took and left.

Kelly was barely out of her teens and still finding herself as a young woman. Yet every mistake she made was public. Every outfit, every change in hair colour was critiqued, its implications endlessly pored over in the tabloid press. Of course Kelly liked to party. She was young, single, so why not? And she worked hard. She wasn't a wannabe, she was a was-a-be. On the outside she was confident and outspoken, happy-go-lucky and with the world at her feet. She has the best smile in the world, and lights up a room the moment she walks in. But she wears her heart on her sleeve. And like every girl of her age she just wanted to fit in, to be accepted.

The group she hung out with – her social circle – were generally much older than she was; some of them already had kids. All they really had in common was their 'fame'. Fortunately she had two really good friends in London who she'd kept in touch with since we'd lived in Welders. She and Sammy started preschool together on the same day, aged three, and have been friends ever since. And then there is Fleur Newman. Her father, Colin, and mother, Mette, could well be said to be our best friends, Ozzy's and mine. They are certainly our oldest friends. Colin worked for my father, and we have known him for forty-plus years.

I didn't really know much about what was going on in Kelly's life. And even if I had, it's doubtful I could have done anything anyway. If I say, 'Don't cross that road, Kel,' she'll not only cross it but she'll stand in the middle and wave her arms. In other words, she's a pea from the maternal pod, both fearless and bloody-minded. She'll fix me with those gorgeous green eyes and tell me *exactly* what she thinks of my latest life choice. But she's also disarmingly tactile and affection-ate, so the next day we'll hug and everything will be fine again.

In the nature of the job, all mothers worry about their children, usually unnecessarily, but when I saw pictures of Kelly in the press looking wrecked, I was really worried. But I was three thousand miles away – what could I do?

It didn't help that I was responsible for her 'fame'. From the moment *The Osbournes* first aired she'd been considered public property, and the reference to 'Ozzy Osbourne's two fat kids' took its toll. I took none of this into consideration when I made the decision to put my kids into the public domain. The truth is, I was throwing them into a lions' den.

The last episode of *The Osbournes* aired in 2005. Although they had been repeated and repeated, requests regularly came in from different networks to get the Osbournes back together again. No way! What made the show great was that the children were teenagers and we all lived under the same roof. It was totally genuine – nothing was invented, nothing was done for camera. Now we had all moved on, and had no intention of going there ever again, and we didn't.

Osbournes Reloaded was an entirely different concept. This wasn't a reality show, it was basically a variety show. We did comedy sketches. We did silly games. Ozzy sang, Kelly sang. It was scripted and rehearsed and filmed over a long period of time (although Ozzy's adherence to the script was minimal). We did filmed segments going around America meeting other families also called Osbourne. Aimee was asked whether she wanted to be involved and, just as before, on the original *The Osbournes*, she said no.

One reason I decided to go ahead was that I recognised it as an opportunity for us to be together. Increasingly we were off doing our own thing. Jack was climbing mountains in obscure corners of the world, Kelly was working in the UK, Ozzy was touring in the Far East, while I was doing a daily talk show in California. This way, we'd be working together for the first time in years, and we'd be getting paid. Finally it was a way of bringing Kelly back home. It was a no-brainer. The show was like a new animal for us, a different experience. It was filmed in front of a live studio audience of 600 people. There were to be six shows, and the whole project would take three months.

Of course, being the Osbournes, this wasn't ordinary variety. It wasn't polite, like *Donny & Marie* or Ant and Dec. The scripts were good, everything was really funny, but it was edgy. The show's researchers scoured the internet for wacky stories. They found a guy who was a serial dater, who claimed to have dated ten women and had sex with each of them on the first night. So they found the girls, who were let in on the joke. Not so the guy – he had just been invited to appear on a new games show. We lined the girls up behind a screen, put him in front of it and when these women he'd slept with for one night only were revealed, he was asked to name them. To give him his credit, he did recognise a few.

Then there were a brother and sister who'd been brought up by their grandmother, who they'd said was always embarrassing them. They were invited to the show and at one point they watched as a naked woman danced to 'Girls, Girls, Girls' by Mötley Crüe. She was behind a backlit screen so you could only see the silhouette. They had no idea who it was, of course. Then when the screen went back, their grandmother was revealed, by now covered up in a dressing gown. At first the kids were mortified, but then they joined in the general hilarity and were on the floor laughing.

Of the six shows, only one was aired. Why? It was

thought to be in poor taste. As indeed it was, but that was the point. What made it all the more surprising was that the guy who commissioned the series also ran the network. In the end the one episode that was broadcast – and then only via a few local affiliates, and only after ten o'clock – did really well, getting audience figures in excess of ten million. The rest were scrapped, and are now gathering dust in some warehouse somewhere, I assume. But there were no hard feelings. It was a great payday, and it's not like our lives were depending on it. You just move on.

The world is much smaller now than it was when I was Kelly's age, and it had been naive of me to imagine that she'd drop all her London friends just because she'd returned to LA. It wasn't long before a boyfriend moved in. She became remote, answering the phone in monosyllables, if she answered at all. Kelly was hibernating. The phone was always engaged. And when Kelly hibernates, she's either depressed or feeling guilty about something.

It was two friends who alerted me to what was really going on. Her house, they said, stank of pot and beer. But was it just him? I couldn't bear it.

I was desperate to say or do something, and fantasised about marching round there, grabbing him by both earlobes and dragging him to the airport and on to a London-bound one-way flight. But I kept putting my head in the sand and telling myself tomorrow, I'll address it tomorrow. I would always put it off. I didn't want to have a fight with my daughter.

Jack was really worried too. He was convinced it wasn't just the numbskull boyfriend, and it was extra hard for him because he worked such a rigid programme with his own sobriety. He has a very dry wit, so his way of dealing with it was to bring it into the conversation, hoping it might permeate the pot fog at Kelly's. But they were both so off their tits, he told me, that they weren't taking anything in. Kelly's response was to call me and say, 'Mummy, do something, will you? Jack's picking on me again.'

Once *Reloaded* was out of the way, Ozzy and I had a really serious talk and came to the conclusion that we needed to stage an intervention with our daughter, to save her from herself. An intervention is where family and friends decide that enough is enough. You go to where they are living and face them with the facts. It's all done in the presence of a trained therapist and there's an exit plan in place – a rehab or clinic of some sort is expecting them. Having discussed the situation with the therapist, and knowing she wouldn't go into rehab of her own volition, he agreed that this was the only way.

I've done interventions before, both with my husband and my son, but Kelly's was by far the worst. Knowing her penchant for the dramatic, I wasn't surprised.

Kelly's house was built in the 1930s by an architect called Peter Bird, and it's way up in the hills. These 'Bird houses', as they are called, are famous. They are usually quite small but always have the most amazing views. From hers, you could see all the way down Sunset Strip to downtown LA. Her actual address was Hollywood Boulevard, but streets in LA are long, and this was old Hollywood – her stretch was a long way from Mann's Chinese Theatre and the Kodak Theatre where the Oscars are held. It was a little gem, all on one level with just one bedroom, dressing area, kitchen/ dining room and living room, with gardens back and front.

So we get there and Ozzy knocks. It was just the two

of us at this stage. It was noon, not a time she would expect us to drop in for a cup of tea or to ask her advice on where to have lunch. The moment she saw us she knew this wasn't a social call. She'd been there before. Twice. And she'd been there when we did an intervention for Jack, and of course for her father.

We eased our way in. The boyfriend was watching TV and Kelly was repeating, 'Look, I'm tired. Can't you see I'm tired?' Gradually the others made their way up the steps and into the house, a host of friends including Melinda, our Australian nanny who was with us when we were shooting *The Osbournes* and who turned into a staunch family friend. Within four minutes the house was full.

The way it works is that the therapist drives the intervention. They're like a referee; there to calm everyone down, to stop the bickering that goes back and forth and to get it to a level where everybody is chatting nicely and saying their bit. That's the idea, anyway. But Kelly wouldn't take it. Within minutes she was throwing herself around the place, shouting and screaming at us to get the hell out.

I saw the panic in her eyes. She was frightened and

ashamed. I could see all of this in her face and my heart was breaking for her. This was my little girl, the sweetest, funniest person ever with a big heart. I could picture her on her swing, with her little welly boots, sucking her thumb, running around the garden with the dogs without a care in the world. Now here she was, embarrassed, frightened, lost. And it wasn't just me. It was the same for Ozzy and Jack. All we wanted to do was help her. She hadn't done anything wrong. She had hurt no one but herself. She was just our little girl, the joy of our lives, and she was hurting herself. And now she was like a caged animal, lashing out. I know in my heart she must have wanted to break down, curl up in a ball and cry. But she's got my front and my strength, so she just lashed out.

'Get out,' she screamed. 'Get out! I'm calling the police.' And she did.

And they came; they had to. She was the householder.

Two uniformed officers arrived, casting a practised eye over the room before their gaze settled on Ozzy, who was pacing around and muttering to no one in particular.

'What seems to be the problem here, ma'am?' one of them asked Kelly.

'These people are in my house and I want them out.'

'Who are they?'

'My mother, my father, my brother . . . '

'It's an intervention,' I explained, and introduced the therapist. Then I talked to them, and then Ozzy talked to them. Eventually they left, agreeing that it was 'a highly personal situation'.

All the time she was repeating, 'Why are you doing this? What have I done? I'm not doing anything wrong.' How do you begin to explain to someone that the only thing they're doing is hurting themselves? By this time I knew that she had been fired by the BBC for not turning up. And yet I know Kelly. The last thing she would want would be to let anyone down. The only person she'd let down was herself. It's like a web you weave to cover up your actions, a web of lies, reasons for not turning up, reasons to justify bad behaviour, and she was so entangled in it she didn't know how to get out.

What she didn't realise is that it's easier to throw in the towel, to own up to what you have done, to become truthful. But it takes years to get there. And once you do, it's freeing. It only comes with maturity, however, and whatever qualities my darling Kelly had, maturity wasn't one of them.

She was like a volcano. Someone would say something and Kelly would erupt. Someone else would speak, she'd calm down and then she would kick off again. It must have gone on for three to four hours. And all the time Kelly was venting her anger on me. Because I was the person closest to her and she knew I'd take it. We'd made arrangements for Kelly to go into Hazelden, a rehab facility in Portland, Oregon. They don't care who you are. It's not a rest home for the rich and famous with paparazzi lurking in the shrubbery. It's a serious, serious treatment centre.

I left towards the end. I couldn't be there to watch Kelly pack a bag, be put in a car and taken to the airport. Because that's what you have to do. You can't say, well, think about it overnight and we'll talk tomorrow, because the addict will run. That was exactly what Jack did when we tried to do an intervention on him when he was seventeen. It was at our house in Malibu and he just legged it, dodging the cars on Pacific Coast Highway, not returning till morning.

_____

I was exhausted, emotionally and physically. My heart felt bruised, just as if I'd been punched. History was repeating itself. An Osbourne was on the skids; only the first names were different.

The next six weeks were hard. Kelly was officially an adult and so her privacy was sacrosanct. When I called the facility I was given no information. 'Kelly Osbourne? We have no record of anyone here of that name.'

Eventually came what's known as family week, the final six days of the programme. I knew how it worked. I was already a veteran; Jack once, Kelly twice and Ozzy God knows how many times.

The therapists change, but otherwise it's the same wherever you are. It's basically an education in the science of addiction, both for the addict and their family. Nobody drinks or does drugs 'because they like it'. Usually it's a screen to hide what's going on inside. And now science has identified a gene that you have or you don't have. But having the gene doesn't mean that you're doomed. The tools are there. All that's needed is the will to use them.

That week was particularly hard for Ozzy, and I

know that he was dreading it and not only because he'd been in treatment himself. One of the first things he was told was that Kelly was in there because of him. Not only because the gene can be hereditary, but also because to her addiction was normal behaviour. And if her daddy could be that way and still be successful and accepted by everyone, then why couldn't she? I knew that it broke his heart that she might be following in his footsteps – he knows how painful and destructive it is. But he finds it hard to verbalise his feelings. He's much better at writing them.

Years ago I decided I would never put myself through family week with Ozzy again. I've had it. He has the tools, and if he chooses not to use them, well, that's his problem. God knows, I've tried. But for my children – when you're a mother, you never give up. I will go every time. They have their whole lives in front of them, and anything I can do to make it easier, I will. So there I was again, in family week.

When I got there, Kelly ran into my arms. She cried, I cried. She apologised for blaming me for everything and for not speaking to me. I understood. What must it be like to grow up in a household where your father is a drunkard? Children learn by example. They had watched him battle with addiction their entire lives. Through it all we'd stuck together. For him, there was no downside. We always took him back; his fans supported him, as did we. His career remained intact. We allowed him to get away with bad and selfish behaviour. We have a co-dependent relationship. As much as he's addicted to alcohol and drugs, I'm addicted to him.

That week, Kelly told Ozzy a few home truths. He was shamed but not cowed. He responded with anger and self-loathing. As I say, he finds it hard to articulate verbally, so he says nothing. It is hugely frustrating and disappointing, but I understand it.

Ozzy's stance with the children has always been, 'I've always provided for you. I've always given you what you've wanted. You've never gone without.' And that continues to be his justification. It's a crock of shit.

You can walk away from a husband, but you can't walk away from your children, whatever they have done.

Now Kelly was out on her own and needed time to adjust, to re-evaluate her life. She was lucky. She had her own home and she was weighing up her options.

She'd shown that she was a performer on the West End stage; she was like, OK, now what?

And then the phone rang. It was *Dancing with the Stars*. Would she be interested?

Dancing with the Stars is the US version of *Strictly Come Dancing*. Even the judges are the same – at least, two of them are, Len Goodman and Bruno Tonioli. In fact, Kelly and I had been approached several years before, but it didn't work out. I had had lessons, and I knew that it was hard, really hard.

Kelly didn't have to think twice. She was in. And it couldn't have been more fortuitous. The timing was perfect. *Dancing with the Stars* is totally involving. She did a month's training, and then it was six days a week as long as you stayed in. It's a huge commitment. It's all or nothing, and it's a complete gift. You learn to dance with the best dancers in the world. And we're not talking a couple of hours a week. When you do *DWTS*, you can't do anything else.

Above all, it gave Kelly a structure. There was no saying, 'Oh, I've got a hair appointment,' or 'I don't feel well.' Once you'd signed up, you were in.

*

Kelly had never done any ballroom dancing before in her life, and she loved it. As for her partner, Louis van Amstel, he couldn't have been better. Like all the best teachers, he was both patient and inspirational. He nurtured her, he gave her confidence at a time in her life when she was feeling she'd fucked everything up. He put her on a path and made her feel good about herself. As far as I am concerned, that show saved her life.

The physical transformation – clearer eyes, dewy skin, weight loss and improved muscle tone – came later, but mentally I saw a change in her almost straight away. Not only was she dancing every day, but she was doing Pilates to strengthen her inner core. Louis was like a life coach for her. He adored her and she adored him. They're still in touch.

She'd call me at 7 a.m. most days during the rehearsal period.

'Hi, Mummy, just calling to say hello before I leave for practice.' She sounded cheerful, *purposeful*. It was a joy to hear. I didn't want to bother her by going down every day to watch, and besides they were in a dance studio getting on with it and didn't want constant interruptions. But after a few weeks of rehearsals, and shortly before the first show aired, she called me as usual in the morning.

'Mum, I really want to show you my dance.'

So I went down to the studio, feeling faintly sick with anticipation. I knew how much it meant to her to get this right.

She was wearing leggings under a long dance skirt, her hair scraped back from her face. The track, 'Trouble' by Ray LaMontagne, filled the room and she started to do the most exquisitely graceful waltz. Oh my God, it was magical, so innocent. I could tell by the look of concentration on her face that she was trying really hard.

I was so overcome that I fell silent. I couldn't trust myself to speak, I just drank it all in: this precious minute and a half of my beautiful daughter dancing her heart out with her professional partner. Just three months earlier, I had been part of an intervention because I was so worried about her well-being, and now here she was, healthy, super-fit, focused and just utterly, utterly gorgeous. Her voice punctuated my reverie.

'Mum, what do you think?' She was staring at me intently.

'Darling, I'm just in awe of you, and so proud.' I had tears in my eyes and a huge lump in my throat.

One week later, she glided out in front of the nation, many of whom had probably read that she'd been in rehab and were thinking, 'Oh, here's the nightmare wild child.' They knew the story and were waiting for something to go wrong, but she just blew them away. When this slight figure in a floor-length, electric-blue ballgown appeared I grasped Ozzy's arm in a flood of emotion. She was so beautiful. And you could see the joy on her face. Then she started dancing. What can I say? Her movements, the way she carried her head, the curve of her back . . . I couldn't believe it. I could see the work, the commitment. By the time she rushed over to see us, Ozzy and I were clutching each other, both in floods of tears.

Just months before she'd been this broken creature, crawling on the ground. And now . . . a glorious butterfly had emerged, to take wing and fly.

It was too much to hope that she would win – I mean, you can't compete with Donny Osmond, who has danced his entire life. But our little Kelly made the final, coming third behind a singer called Maya, who was also a dancer.

Everything about that show was nurturing and empowering, and she has learnt a new skill which will last her all her life. And from the moment she took her final bow, the phone hasn't stopped ringing.

4

No Rest for the Wicked

Ozzy and Black Sabbath guitarist Tony Iommi in 1978.

A few years ago I had this idea that we would slow down a bit. I even thought Ozzy might retire when he reached sixty. That was the plan, at least.

What was I thinking? Ozzy, stop working? It's about as likely as me stuffing the red hair dye at the back of the bathroom cabinet and going au naturel while tending my herbaceous borders. It ain't gonna happen.

Ozzy turned sixty on 3 December 2008, while we were in the middle of filming *Osbournes Reloaded*. I had planned a surprise party for him in Las Vegas, but first I had to get him there; not easy with someone who hates leaving the house unless it's for a recording studio or stage. After much deliberation, I told him that we had to fly to Vegas two days before to film with a family for the show's 'The Osbournes meet the Osbournes' slot. This went down quite badly.

'Fucking hell, Sharon, what a shit way to spend my birthday.' I think he probably suspected all was not as it seemed, but he moaned the whole way there anyway.

I was telling the truth. He was going to meet a family called the Osbournes. His own. I had arranged for a crowd of family and friends, including his sisters, Gillian, Jean and Iris, to fly out from the UK to surprise him. When we reached the hotel, we walked in and there they all were. Jack, Aimee and Kelly came, of course, and so did Louis and Jessica, his children from his first marriage. It was really fantastic, everyone being together, because it hadn't happened that much over the years.

Ozzy's relationship with each of his sisters is good, but he's particularly close to his oldest sister, Jean. It's like she has become the mother he never really had. The pecking order in their family, in terms of birth, is Jean, Iris, Gillian, Paul, Ozzy and Tony. Jean is the one he speaks to regularly, usually every week, and she tells him what the rest of the family are up to. He doesn't see much of his brothers because they all have such different lives now. There's no bad feeling, it's just that they have grown apart. It happens, particularly when you don't even live in the same country.

It was fantastic that Louis and Jessica came, and Ozzy was thrilled as it was a great opportunity for them to spend much needed time together. For Jack it was a heaven-sent opportunity, and he took it. He was filming a documentary on his father called *God Bless Ozzy Osbourne*. Jack bankrolled it himself. He invested in his own equipment, cameras, hired a cameraman and a sound guy and followed Ozzy around the world for a couple of years. It debuted at the Tribeca Film Festival in New York, sold to Showtime and was the most-watched documentary on the network. It made him money and laid the foundation stone for a career behind the camera instead of in front of it.

Ozzy wasn't a good dad to the children of his first marriage because he was absent so much of the time. It's easier now that they're adults with children themselves, and the relationship is better, but it's still slightly distant because of all those lost years that you can never make up.

Jessica has three children and Louis has two, so Ozzy

has five grandchildren living in the UK. But again, you have to have regular contact with little people to build up a closeness. You can't walk into their lives on birthdays and at Christmas and expect them to open their arms for a hug and say, 'Hello, Granddad.' Unfortunately for every grandparent in the same position, it's just what happens when your grandchildren grow up on the other side of the world. It's not anyone's fault, it's just how it is.

It's a long-distance relationship both physically and emotionally, and Ozzy knows that. That's why he wants to try and do things differently with Pearl.

The celebrations were spread over three nights. The first was family night. After the initial surprise of finding his entire family in Las Vegas, Ozzy began to enjoy himself. A further surprise awaited him when we took everyone to see the Beatles tribute show, *Love*. Ozzy is a lifelong fan, and he was in his element. Afterwards we went backstage where the entire cast sang 'Happy Birthday'.

The next night's treat was at Caesar's Palace, in the Colosseum, where Bette Midler was performing her spectacular *The Showgirl Must Go On*.

No Rest for the Wicked

When Ozzy and I were first working together, back in 1979, I would take him to see iconic artistes' shows. I wanted him to watch how they performed, how they dealt with an audience. I was educating him on performance and production. And one of these performers was Bette Midler. She was playing at the Universal Amphitheatre in Los Angeles, so I took Ozzy along, together with the guitar player Gary Moore, who I managed at the time. So it's a beautiful midsummer night in an open-air theatre and we have front-row seats. Unsurprisingly, we're late. We're walking down the central aisle and Bette Midler is on stage singing, sees us and stops mid-number.

'Well, there always has to be one shmuck who gets in late and walks in while I'm singing, and here's the shmuck,' she says, pointing at Ozzy. In fact, Ozzy didn't even know who Bette Midler was. He was a working-class kid from Birmingham and his taste in music didn't extend to musical theatre. She peers at him with his long hair and eccentric style of dress – obviously rather different to the sartorial tastes of the rest of the audience – and goes, 'Are you sure you're at the right show?' And Ozzy dies of embarrassment.

He doesn't know what to do. I, on the other hand, am dying of laughter, along with everyone else. Ozzy is OK, but on the way back to the apartment he never stops saying, 'Where are we, Sharon? I want to go home . . . '

Fast-forward thirty-plus years. Again, we're in the front row and Bette says nothing, but comes down among the audience in the middle of a song, takes Ozzy's hand and sings to him. He certainly knows who she is this time, and he absolutely loves it. After the show, we go backstage and sit in a little anteroom. There is a knock at the door, and in comes an enormous birthday cake, wheeled by the diva in person, still wearing her showgirl costume and full make-up, singing 'Happy Birthday, dear Ozzy' as it has never been sung before.

The next day was his actual birthday, and it was back to Caesar's Palace, this time to Il Mulino, where I had booked the whole restaurant. Because it wasn't just family any more. The numbers were swollen by friends who had flown in from all over the world. It was a lot to take in, but he was bowled over.

As my special birthday present, I had a ring made

out of a diamond solitaire Ozzy had once bought me when the children were small but which I had never worn because it had been a guilty gift following some really bad behaviour on his part, when he actually thumped me. The diamond was beautiful, however, so I decided on a reincarnation and had it reset on a thick gold band with big diamond crosses at either side. Ozzy will tell anyone who'll listen that he doesn't particularly like jewellery, but take a look at him on any given day and he's covered in the stuff. Rings, bracelets and always one, sometimes two or three, necklaces, usually involving crucifixes, skulls and diamonds. I don't like jewellery, my arse. Anyway, he loved it. He also loved the whole birthday shebang. I mean, talk about doing it in style. Las Vegas for three days . . . 'I don't usually like surprises,' he said, 'but this one was different,' adding, 'besides, you don't like surprises either.'

'How the fuck would you know?' I said. 'You've never *planned* a surprise for me in your entire life.' He has certainly given me plenty of surprises, but unfortunately not of the pleasant kind.

*

The milestone birthday over, Ozzy's thoughts, and therefore mine, as his manager, turned to what the next decade would hold for him, work-wise.

Ozzfest, the annual heavy-metal festival we had established in 1996, was still going strong, but for Ozzy, Black Sabbath was never far from his mind. There's an invisible thread that holds them together. Sabbath has been a huge part of Ozzy's life.

He was at school with Tony Iommi, Sabbath's guitar player. Right from the start they were chalk and cheese. Tony had much, much more confidence. His parents owned a grocery shop, while Ozzy's parents were both factory workers. Tony – an only child – always had enough to eat. Ozzy was one of six, and the only way to be sure of getting fed was to get to the table first. A can of Campbell's condensed soup and half a loaf of bread often had to make do for all the family.

After leaving school, Ozzy worked in a factory tuning car horns, and then in a slaughterhouse. But at the age of nineteen, he put an ad in the local music shop saying that his name was Ozzy Zigg, that he was a singer and was looking for a band. Tony and another local boy called Bill Ward turned up at Ozzy's house

With my crazy, beautiful family, hosting the 2008 Brit Awards at Earl's Court, London.

Dannii and I put on a united front for her first live *X Factor* show, but backstage it was a completely different – and very explosive – story.

Only weeks later, the alliances on the judging panel were clear for everyone to see.

As if the bad atmosphere on *The X Factor* wasn't enough to deal with, Minnie – my best friend and companion for so many years – died in 2008. I was heartbroken.

Me, Minnie and Maggie in our glory days.

This frame originally held a picture of Ozzy meeting his hero Paul McCartney. The inscription now reads: *Minnie was bigger than any Beatle. I love you. Ozzy.*

Bella is now top dog, and I couldn't ask for a more loyal – or a cuter – friend.

The Osbournes (2002): The show that kicked off this whole crazy ride. We all have mixed feelings about the series now.

The Osbournes Reloaded (2009): The show that I hoped would bring the family back together, both on and offscreen. You can see from our expressions that it was not the happy experience I was hoping for.

Kelly, recently emerged from rehab, practises her *Dancing with the Stars* routine with partner Louis van Amstel in 2009.

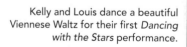

Kelly and Louis dance a beautiful Viennese Waltz for their first *Dancing with the Stars* performance.

Ozzy and I were so incredibly proud of Kelly, and delighted to see her happy and healthy after her recent troubles.

Kelly and her fiancé, Matthew Mosshart.

Ozzy celebrates his 60th birthday in Las Vegas. His cake featured a fabulous photo of him as an angelic-looking little boy.

With Aimee, Ozzy, Kelly and Jack at Ozzy's 60th.

Ward, Iommi, Osbourne, Butler: The original band line-up in 1970 (above), and at a press conference with producer Rick Rubin (below, far right) announcing their reunion in 2011.

and knocked at the door. Tony played lead guitar and Bill was the drummer. Ozzy didn't play an instrument, but he had his own PA system bought on the never-never, his father acting as guarantor. Even owning your own microphone was rare – a whole system was magic, and this was why they'd come. When Ozzy opened the door, Tony said to Bill, 'Oh shit. I was at school with him.' Ozzy just said, 'Oh, shit.' Tony had been the school bully. Together with Terry Butler, always known as Geezer, this unlikely group of Brummie lads became pioneers in the genre of harder-edged music.

Ten years later, in 1979, Ozzy was fired and signed away his share of the name for a paltry $25,000. He was off his head with drink and drugs and couldn't have read a bus ticket, let alone masterminded an exit deal from the band he'd been such an integral part of.

They were then based in LA, under contract to my father. I was doing the day-to-day and had rented them a house in Bel Air, where I'd turned the garage into a rehearsal room.

In those days you didn't think about the implications of future earnings. Nobody thought two years ahead, let alone thirty or forty. At that time, no one had been in the rock 'n' roll business for more than twenty years. Ozzy was flat broke and just wanted out, for whatever money he could get, and that's what happened. Eventually, Geezer did the same thing and so did Bill. It all went to Tony. He ended up owning one hundred per cent of the Black Sabbath name.

Let's not forget, these were four working-class lads from Birmingham, so they weren't suddenly going to become business geniuses when it came to a severance deal. And besides, there was a period afterwards when Tony did so many reincarnations of the band with different people that the name wasn't worth a great deal anyway. It became completely devalued.

Strangely, I was a friend of Tony Iommi's long before I got to know Ozzy well when he produced an album for my father's record label, Jet Records, by a band called Quartz. My father had tried to sign Sabbath back in 1970, and that's when I saw them at the Marquee and was blown away. It wasn't to be: they were hijacked by Don's assistant and a bodyguard, who went on to make a fortune with them.

Even though my father never forgave Sabbath for doing the dirty on him, he was a businessman and when

Quartz said they wanted Tony Iommi to produce their album, Don was more than happy. Suddenly we were on talking terms again, and that's how, in late 1978, early 1979, Sabbath came back to ask my father for management. And of course he accepted.

When Ozzy was fired by the band in 1979, I took him under my wing. He was a real talent, a charismatic performer with great wit and likeability. I'd been unhappy at how he'd been treated – basically bullied – by them. The way I saw it, Ozzy had spent his life being bullied, at home, at school by Tony, among others, and now by Black Sabbath, because he was an insecure people-pleaser and everyone took advantage of that.

Sometime before, I had introduced Tony Iommi to Ronnie Dio (formerly of Rainbow) who then replaced Ozzy in Sabbath. So while Sabbath were in the studio doing a new album with Ronnie, Ozzy was in West Hollywood nursing his wounds and licking his paws. Tony and the gang didn't like the fact that my father and I were still looking after him. They expected us to pull the plug. I didn't see the need, so in the end they decided to leave us, going with another manager. It was that continuous on-off relationship my father had had with Black Sabbath taking yet another turn.

My job then was to find Ozzy a band so that he could write a new album and go into the studio on his own account. And the rest is history.

Over the years, Ozzy would play with Sabbath on and off. After he was fired, Sabbath did two studio albums and then a live record with Ronnie Dio. Then Geezer left, selling his portion of the name back to Tony. There is only a finite number of good musicians playing in Ozzy's genre, and Geezer is one of the best bassists in hard rock. It wasn't long before he was playing with Ozzy again, in Ozzy's band, and when Ozzy was playing with another bassist, Geezer would go back to whatever formation Tony had come up with.

Then, from 1997 until 2005, if a project came up for Sabbath in which Ozzy was involved, I would manage it. The name Sabbath gradually began to get its credibility back. Too many reincarnations had put the name in the toilet. Without the original members, it had flat-lined and had been on life support. And as far as Black Sabbath's merchandising was concerned, it had no clout in the marketplace. Merchandise is not an add-on in this world. It's a central part of the business.

From 1998 on, I took over responsibility for running the merchandising, cutting deals, approving the artwork and the rest of it. As the internet and social media grew in importance, I registered BlackSabbath. com as a domain name. All of this took time, effort and money.

In 2005, the British Rock and Roll Hall of Fame was inaugurated. It had existed in the States for many years. Ozzy was asked to be among the first artists to be inducted. He was touring with Black Sabbath when the invitation came, and I suggested that they induct Sabbath at the same time, and they agreed. Ozzy played at the induction with his own band, and also with Sabbath – with all the original members.

I had been lobbying for years to get them inducted into the US Hall of Fame, writing letters to everyone on the committee, so when it was agreed, in 2006, it was great news. It was an acknowledgement that Sabbath were now accepted by the mainstream. And, as is traditional, they were asked to play at the induction ceremony. Tony refused.

If he didn't want to perform, then that was his prerogative. But it was strange. It made Sabbath the only band still alive and working never to have performed at their own induction.

The night before the ceremony, to be held at the Waldorf Astoria Hotel in New York, we'd also been offered a special one-off gig at a small venue in New York City for a fee of one million dollars, to be split equally among the four. Again, Tony refused. No excuse: he just didn't want to do it, he said. Again, this wasn't a catastrophe for us or the other guys. But it was odd. You don't want to earn $250,000 for an hour's work? More power to you.

One week later, we found out why. Tony had got Sabbath back with Ronnie Dio.

Even though Ozzy had been touring with Sabbath at the time, and I was in regular contact with Tony's manager, nothing had been mentioned. But as Tony owned the Sabbath name, he could do whatever he wanted.

So I'm like, OK, fine. Knock yourselves out. I asked for a meeting with Tony's manager where I informed him that, if they went out with Ronnie Dio under the name Black Sabbath, I would sue. Given the band's recent line-up, people would naturally assume that it was Ozzy they were paying to see on tour. After all, this was just days after Sabbath's induction into the US Rock and Roll Hall of Fame, which had got global coverage.

I also told him that I was going to sue for Ozzy's portion of the name back. I was still handling Sabbath's merchandising, and all offers that came in for licensing for any of the music came through my office.

After everything they had been through, personally and professionally, nobody was man enough to turn around to Ozzy and say, 'We want to go in another direction.' They were acting like schoolboys, taking it back years, decades. Ozzy had a solo career, anyway. So why not be up front about it? Why not be respectful, out of courtesy if nothing else?

To cut a long story short, Tony Iommi did the right thing. They did go out with Ronnie Dio, they did play and they made an album, but all under the name Heaven and Hell. Which was absolutely fine for everyone, and we wished them well and we all got on with our lives.

Tragically, Ronnie Dio died of cancer in 2010.

Although people imagined that we must have been at each other's throats, nothing could have been further from the truth. There was nothing personal in this. We had no resentment against Ronnie Dio – none of it was his doing. But the truth is that, had they gone out under the Black Sabbath name, then the history of the band's latest incarnation would never have happened.

Back in early 2010 – way before Ronnie died – the managers of the four original members started talking about the band – Black Sabbath – doing an album. While they were all great musicians, in my view Ozzy had become the face of the band. Yes, I'm his wife and I absolutely idolise him but I'm also a businesswoman. I had spent the last twelve years building up Sabbath's merchandising arm, monitoring the business. I knew their worth with Ozzy and without Ozzy. The reality was that Ozzy had a stable solo career. As it stood, if any of the band's images were used, they would each get a twenty-five per cent cut, but if it was just the band's name, it all went to Tony. This seemed odd to say the least.

'We're only doing the album if Ozzy gets back a share of the Black Sabbath name,' I told Tony's manager.

Tony said no.

'Right. Well then, in that case, we're going to sue you.'

I told Geezer and Bill that we were going to court to try and get back a slice of the band's name, and asked them if they wanted to join us in the lawsuit. Politically it was a difficult situation for them. Geezer was still working with Tony. They had also asked Bill to be in Heaven and Hell but, for whatever reason, it hadn't worked out. The upshot was that they both said no. So I lawyered up and set the ball rolling.

Two months later, Tony moved to get the suit dismissed on the basis that it was 'an effort to rewrite long-settled history'. This got thrown out of court.

We settled in July 2010 with Ozzy owning his rightful portion of the name. It had been a long, expensive and emotionally draining process, and I personally got very bad press from it, but I couldn't give a shit as I was doing the right thing both for my husband and my family. Because long after Ozzy and I are gone, people will still be wearing Black Sabbath T-shirts and buying posters and other memorabilia. And it's only right that some of the profits should be passed on to our family.

It's Ozzy's heritage. Ultimately we're happy with the settlement, and so is Tony. And that's all that matters.

The curious thing is that, throughout all the legal battles, Tony and Ozzy and Geezer always kept up a friendly dialogue, never discussing business, keeping it only to personal stuff and music, which says a lot about them all – and it's part of what makes them so wonderfully strange.

5

In My Opinion

Sharing a joke with young Mr Bieber.

In My Opinion

I count Louis Walsh as a *proper* friend, not one of those 'showbiz' ones that air-kiss you at parties while looking over your shoulder for someone more interesting.

After I quit *The X Factor*, we stayed in regular touch, talking on the phone at least once a week from wherever we were in the world. We still do. It's been a long friendship, and Ozzy loves him too. We know each other so well. We can be at dinner with other people, and if one of them says something that's a bit up their own arse, or whatever, we sort of glance at each other and know we're thinking *exactly* the same thing. If he comes to LA, we hang out, and likewise if we're both in London at the same time.

One day, in early 2010, he called me.

'Sharon, how do you fancy coming over to Ireland to do judges' house with me this summer?'

It wasn't his 'house' at all, it was some Irish castle hotel. But it looked like a really lovely place when I checked it out online, and I adore hanging out with Louis, so how hard could it be? I was over the moon that he'd asked and said yes immediately. I would have walked on water to get there because I knew we'd have such a great time. And we did. It was just him and me, sifting through the over-twenty-fives group, and it was two days of non-stop laughter. I barely slept because, once filming had finished, we were up most of the night chatting and putting the world to rights, and then of course it was a painfully early start again the next day.

A couple of people asked me at the time if it bothered me that I wasn't one of the main judges, but I can honestly say, hand on heart, that it didn't. That type of thing never bothers me. Who cares if you're having fun? It was largely the same crew and producers, so it was like going back to a family but with none of the responsibility. I just went in, got a taste of it again and left. It was fantastic. Obviously, Louis had to get clearance from Simon and all the senior production people to ask me, and they all agreed to it. But he wanted to ask me again the following year, and Simon said no! I never found out why, but Louis ended up with Sinitta.

A couple of days having a laugh in Ireland was just what I needed. I was still recovering from a very different TV experience. In March 2010 I'd headed to New York to take part in *Celebrity Apprentice* on behalf of my colon cancer programme.

In the American version, the Alan Sugar role is taken by property magnate Donald Trump, who probably owns half of New York City. He's a fabulously eccentric character; I have only ever met him socially, but he has always been great to me and my family. I had been approached by NBC, the network that airs *America's Got Talent*, asking if I would like to take part. Just as with the British version, the show entices celebrities with the promise of large amounts of money that they can earn for their nominated charity. So I think to myself, what a great way to raise awareness and money for the colon cancer programme that I run at Cedars-Sinai hospital in Los Angeles.

My colon cancer programme enables people to get free testing. We don't do research; it's more like a helping hand, enabling patients to get to and from treatment as well as providing other kinds of practical help, using volunteers.

The show involves a solid month of filming, six days a week, so it's a big commitment. But I thought it would be good to do. If you get through to the final, you can raise nearly a million dollars, so that's all I thought about when it came to saying yes or no. I had never watched the show, not a single episode. I'd seen the ads, but of course that's just a montage of rapid-fire clips. I had absolutely no idea what I was getting myself into. Silly, silly me.

It's a game, of course it is, but this was gladiatorial combat. I didn't know that I was to be pitched against the other contestants and goaded into believing that everyone is out to get you. As it was for charity, I imagined it would be more supportive and laid-back, so I went into it in total innocence and with a warm, fuzzy feeling of loveliness towards everyone . . . that lasted for about five fucking minutes. It was a vipers' nest.

There were seven men and seven women. On the

women's team, there was Holly Robinson Peete, an American actress and singer; former wrestler Maria Kanellis; Olympic gold-medal swimmer Summer Sanders; Victoria's Secret model Selita Ebanks; comedienne Carol Leifer and singer Cyndi Lauper, who turned out to be the one saving grace. I absolutely loved her. I had met Cyndi, but this experience brought us much closer together. I had also met Holly, though I didn't know her well. The rest of the team were total strangers.

It was horrible. Horrible, horrible, horrible. One minute you're there thinking it's going to be a bit of fun, the next you're running across the city in a muck sweat thinking, Fucking hell, what have I got myself into?

And the producers wanted you to start bickering with each other, as it makes better telly. They would get you on your own and tell you that one of your team-mates had just said something derogatory and inevitably you would become paranoid, thinking, Bloody hell, did they *really* say that? It did my head in – I just hated it.

From day one, everyone started to make allies, plotting in corners about how they were going to bring you down. At one point, some of the other women had a go at Cyndi, who was very passionate, very animated and, shock horror, had an opinion. She was doing the show to support a gay charity and was very determined about doing well to raise funds for it, and for some reason the others started giving her a hard time and taking the piss.

So I said, 'Listen, this is Cyndi Lauper you're talking about, who the *fuck* are you? Don't be so disrespectful to this woman.' I became her protector, in a way, because she's a lovely person with a huge heart and there she was being ridiculed for effect on a bloody TV show. I wasn't having it. I made it very clear that despite their nefarious efforts to get more airtime and to gain notoriety by being bitchy, it was all going to end up on the cutting-room floor because they were fucking nobodies compared to Cyndi. I think it's fair to say that we weren't getting on as a team.

We were miked up the entire time, and so the whole world got to hear us constantly sniping at each other. I don't get it. When men compete, they are very straightforward about it; it's rarely personal. But women so often seem to get behind-the-back mean. It's a fatal flaw of our gender. Cyndi kept saying to all of us, 'It's just a TV show, don't take this personally,' but we didn't listen, we all took the bait. More fool us.

I came within seconds of walking out several times a day, but there were the potential winnings to consider. How could I give up that chance? I'd have been called a quitter, and rightly so. But God, it was a tough show to do. It was a total guilt trip because they knew that you wouldn't walk out on the opportunity to help others – it totally messed with our heads.

We were staying at the Trump International Hotel and had to be in front of Donald by bloody 7 a.m. each day. There was no time to wake up properly or even have a proper breakfast: a takeaway coffee and muffin in a bag were thrust into our hands to eat on the way.

Sometimes we were working through until 1 a.m. then getting up again a few hours later, so it was punishing stuff. It seemed to me that they were deliberately wearing us down to make us vulnerable and tearful. I hated it, and throughout every last, soul-destroying second of doing it, I just thought of the money I would raise for my charity. Otherwise, it would have been *hasta la* bye-bye.

Tasks included writing a radio commercial for a

plumbing firm and designing the interior of an apartment. (I was thrilled to win that one!) I reached the
final three out of fourteen, at which point we had to
become a personal trainer for a day, getting people in
and motivating them to do a workout. We literally had
to pull members of the public off the street and persuade
them to come and be filmed doing exercises, then call
all the famous people we knew and get them to sponsor
us. You had to raise money for every task, so it was hideously embarrassing having to ring your friends and put
them on the spot by asking for donations. I hate asking
people for money, even for charity. Hate it.

For the first task we had to run a restaurant, and I got
everyone I knew in New York to come along. God, it
was hell. By the end of the series, I should think every
time one of my friends saw my name flash up on their
phone, they just switched the bloody thing off. Those
who accidentally answered probably wanted to say
'Fuck off'.

I raised about $165,000 for the workout assignment,
but Holly beat me by $50,000 because she found one
big sponsor who came in at the last minute. Until that
point, we were running neck and neck.

When Donald fired me, he said it was because he didn't feel I was strong enough for the next assignment, which was designing a new flavour for a Snapple drink, for fuck's sake! But as I left that famous boardroom for the last time, all I could think was, Thank fuck for that, now I can go home.

Even though I wanted to win it for my charity, it was tough because I didn't want that to mean that Holly would lose out on raising money for hers. It was a truly invidious situation. Her father has Parkinson's disease and her teenage son has autism, so she set up the HollyRod Foundation to offer help to families living with those conditions. The two finalists were Holly and Bret Michaels of the band Poison. Bret is lovely, and I adore him, but he got very sick after we had filmed all the challenges and returned home complaining of a severe headache. He suffered a brain haemorrhage, and was in hospital for several days before returning to New York to film the finale, when he won a huge amount of money for his chosen charity, the American Diabetes Association.

On camera during the finale Donald said that he had spoken to Bret's doctors. 'They didn't want you to be here tonight. At all. Believe me, not at all. Are you risking your life being here? This is a lot of pressure.' Quick as a shot Bret came back, 'Lately it seems like me just standing up is risking my life.'

I knew just how he felt. Once again, I had said yes to something because I thought people might think badly of me if I didn't do it, and once again I regretted it. Still, at least this time I could console myself that it was for charity and that I would surely go to heaven.

If I can only stop fucking swearing.

If reality shows are the most life-sapping way to earn a crust in show business, then filming adverts must surely rank as the easiest. It's big money, they usually take only one or two days to film and, if the premise and script are good, they don't damage your reputation. They might even enhance it.

The Super Bowl is the annual championship of the NFL, the American football league. It's their equivalent of the Cup Final, and a huge event in the US sporting calendar. But it also attracts millions of TV viewers who have no interest in sport because of the big half-time show and the hilarious, budget-busting ads that run in the breaks. It's part of the tradition that all the major companies pay a fortune to do a special advert that's really over the top and funny.

Ozzy had done one years before, for Pepsi Twist, which showed Kelly and Jack holding the can before turning into Donny and Marie Osmond before Ozzy's horrified eyes, and it had gone down really well. Then, in 2011, a marketing company approached us about Ozzy doing an ad for a big US electronics firm called Best Buy. It was a really funny idea, and we jumped at it.

The premise was that new technology moves so fast, it's hard for old rockers like Ozzy to keep up. The set was like a space station, and they had Ozzy in an intergalactic suit like something out of *Star Wars*.

In the ad, he faces the camera, holds up a mobile phone and says, 'Welcome to 4G!' before someone shouts, 'Cut!' and an assistant wanders into shot to tell him that it's now been updated to 5G. Of course, Ozzy being Ozzy, he can't grasp this and he keeps getting it wrong before muttering, 'How many bloody Gs are there?'

Enter stage left Justin Bieber, also in an intergalactic

suit, who comes up to Ozzy and says, 'I'll take it from here,' before doing a little dance and declaring, 'It's Bieber, 6G fever,' the message being that technology moves fast, so don't get left behind. The ad ends with me and Ozzy standing on the sidelines watching Justin, and me saying, 'What's a Six G?' and Ozzy replying, 'What the fuck's a Bieber?'

Funny, right? Except that the last bit wasn't a spoof, because Ozzy genuinely had absolutely no idea who Justin Bieber was.

Justin was sixteen at the time and still looked really young with a cute teen haircut. He was so sweet and polite to everyone, and he turned up on time and was generally very eager to please. I met his mum, who seemed to be a lovely woman, and his manager was there too, overseeing things.

Many times you see kids that get an astonishing level of fame quite quickly, and they don't always handle it well. They crash and burn. But at the time, I remember thinking that Justin was surrounded by good people and seemed very grounded.

In the three years since then, his image has changed. Three years seems like nothing to us, but when you're sixteen to nineteen it seems an eternity. So what we have here is basically a child entertainer who is a world-wide pop star. He's very talented, very charismatic and to all his fans he represents youth, great pop music and fun. Unfortunately for Justin, growing up in the public eye is hideous, but even more so for someone in his position. Historically, entertainers his age in pop music have a short shelf time. It comes with the territory, especially when you don't write your own songs and your audience is made up of teenage girls. Their taste in music changes just as their taste in fashion does – and what does that do for people like Justin?

I've been pretty hard on him when we've discussed him on *The Talk*, but looking at him as a mother, my heart goes out to him. Yes, he's hugely successful and making millions for everyone around him. And this business is so cruel, so hard, that I'm afraid it might eat him up and shit him out. As a manager looking in, sure his people are doing a great job. But as a *mother*, I see this nineteen-year-old pop star who sings 'Baby Baby Baby', who wants to be a tough guy, hanging with his mates and causing trouble as most normal nineteen-year-old boys do. But I'm sure his record company and advisers want to hear another 'Baby Baby Baby', so there must be conflict within him. I sympathise, because it's the hardest thing to be a child entertainer and then make that transition to grown-up artist. But Justin Timberlake managed it. He is the model Justin Bieber should be focusing on.

The boy I met doing the Best Buy commercial was delightful and under the brash exterior of someone now trying to be an edgy 'bro' (but who is actually just being a pain in the arse), I still see that childlike innocence and I hope he comes out the other side of all this in one piece.

No doubt after writing this I will attract the legendary opprobrium of Justin's devoted followers, the Beliebers. Bring it on, girls. In a couple of years' time, when you're slightly older and a whole lot wiser, you'll see my point.

The other day, I was reading an article about Harry Styles from One Direction writing some solo material and I thought, Here we go, it's Robbie Williams all over again.

I have to hand it to Simon on this one. When he

first started *The X Factor* he was constantly saying, 'I want to find an 'N Sync, I want to find a Spice Girls.' Oh my God, he really did with One Direction. They are, at this moment, the biggest boy band in the world and they came from little old *X Factor* UK. Basically, they're five little boys who look great, with great personalities too, but OK singers. I don't think they would have made it alone, but you put them together and you create magic.

Again, we have musical history repeating itself. We've seen this kind of success in the past with the Jacksons, the Osmonds, Backstreet Boys, Bros, Take That, the Bay City Rollers, 'N Sync, New Kids on the Block and let's not forget the fabulous Spice Girls. Each group represented their generation, their time. Each had amazing worldwide success, generating millions, but having a specific shelf life. Boy bands are like athletes. Their careers are like a flame. They burn strong and bright but only for a short period of time. Also, in any group you're dealing with different personalities of course, and history tells us again that there's a honeymoon period and after that, because of egos, musical differences, maturity or immaturity, people change and they want different things. How often have we seen the most popular one or the cheekiest one leave to pursue a solo career? Some of the bands I have mentioned have reunited in recent years and have had success for a second time but I think it's only Justin Timberlake, Robbie Williams, Gary Barlow and Michael Jackson who can truly say they made it on their own. Based on past musical history you would give One Direction another three years and – being the betting woman I am – I would say Harry Styles will be the first one to leave the group for a solo career. Let's see. It's fascinating being an outsider looking in on these scenarios.

When you consider the 60s club, each of them is a pioneer in the industry. Elton John, Rod Stewart, Bruce Springsteen, the Rolling Stones, Robert Plant, Ozzy, Billy Joel, Cyndi Lauper. Each one of them is a quint-essential artist who represents their genre. When they are gone, who will take over? These are icons of their individual musical genres, unique and irreplaceable.

Of the newer artists, Adele stands out to me in the same way. She is a breath of fresh air in the music industry. She had her first hit record when she was just eighteen, her first album was nominated for a Grammy and her second album *won* the Grammy. She's an artist who goes way beyond any particular demographic; her music speaks a universal language. At a time when many stars in the industry couldn't sell albums any more, she came along and proved a point. You can still sell tens of millions of albums worldwide. Her audience ranges from kids to pensioners.

Artists like Adele come once in a lifetime. She arrived at a time when music executives were screaming about illegal downloading, music streaming services, YouTube, the demise of MTV as a music channel, the prevalence of iTunes leading to record stores closing by the thousands. And Adele proved that if the music was right, it would sell. Taylor Swift – who appeals particularly to a younger audience – also came out of nowhere and sold millions.

The thing that always amazes me about this industry is that, decade after decade, people make slamming statements like, 'Heavy metal is over,' 'Grunge is over,' 'Boy bands are over,' 'There is no record industry any more and DJs are the new rock stars.' And then from virtually nowhere you get these ground-breaking artists who change all the rules and the face of the industry.

It's amazing what one artist like Adele can do for a record label. The fact is, there are no rules, there are no standards, there are no 'ABC's and that's what makes the record industry so exciting, sexy and innovative. There's always a new generation with a new talent pool waiting to be discovered.

Kelly works as an international fashion correspondent on *Fashion Police*, hosted by the brilliantly acerbic Joan Rivers, famous for poking fun at Hollywood celebrities as well as herself. As the title suggests, the idea behind the show is to critique what famous people wear to various red-carpet events, so if, like Lady Gaga, you have a fondness for wacky outfits, then it's fairly likely you're going to attract attention. Some might say you're actively seeking that attention.

At the 2012 Grammy Awards, Gaga skipped the red-carpet bit but appeared inside wearing a bizarre dominatrix outfit that caused quite a stir. It had a mesh veil that covered her face and a long flap at the front that covered her stomach area. Her breasts seemed larger than usual, and Kelly speculated that she might be pregnant.

In My Opinion

Well, that off-the-cuff comment unleashed a torrent of abuse against Kelly on Twitter, from Gaga's fans – or 'little monsters' as Gaga calls them. Some of it was really nasty stuff, saying that Kelly should be raped or murdered.

Obviously, she was upset, not to mention disturbed, by this – and it didn't let up. Their threatening, horrible messages continued to come. It was like a tsunami and went on and on and on.

As I know Gaga's manager, I contacted him and asked if she could just post something on her website to tell her fans to lighten up on Kelly. Gaga is the self-proclaimed poster child for anti-bullying.

She and I had actually met. We had been moderators with Cyndi Lauper for the make-up company MAC, when they were doing the Viva Glam campaign, and we had hosted a press conference too and had a great day together. As I'd also met her a couple of times with Elton John, I didn't think there would be a problem.

Her manager said, 'I'm on it,' but I didn't hear from him again and nothing appeared on her website. Then the comments got worse and worse, to the point where Kelly called me in floods of tears.

'Mummy, it's just never-ending.'

Eventually, in May 2013, Kelly did a magazine inter-view in which she mentioned that Gaga's fans were some of the worst for bullying her and that, in her view, the star was a hypocrite for not stopping it. In the mean-time I emailed the manager, politely reminding him that I had asked before and nothing was done, but could Gaga please tell her fans to cool it with Kelly, as it was becoming really uncomfortable and upsetting for her. I sent him a link to a fan blog that suggested my daughter 'needs to kill herself', and reminding him that Gaga was a vocal campaigner against bullying:

Vince,

I'm leaving it in your hands to do the right thing here. One tweet from Gaga can change this whole situation. I'm not asking her to deal with this directly but if she could tweet something to her fans about being more respectful that may end this. I'm sure she doesn't condone her fans saying such hideously offensive things.

Wishing you and your family the best in 2013.

All the best,

Sharon

In My Opinion

Within one hour Gaga posted a reply to Kelly on her website, signed off by her and her mother Cynthia, as co-founders of the anti-bullying charity, the Born This Way Foundation. It was a pompous statement about promoting positivity, criticising Kelly for 'choosing a less compassionate path' in her job on *Fashion Police*, and saying that she, Gaga, was a 'woman that cares deeply for humanity'.

However, it seems that her humanity doesn't appear to extend to telling her fans to back off from sending relentlessly bullying comments to a young woman so obviously distressed by them. She could easily have done that, but instead she said that, while she actively discourages the fans from negativity and violence in general, she can't control them.

I'm afraid that, as the reply was from her mother too, I saw red and thought, That's it, the gloves are off. If *your* mother's in it, I am too.

She may well have been bullied at school and been the outcast, but she was also the little rich kid from New York that got everything she fucking wanted. She should know better.

So I responded in an open letter and went to town on her, saying she was a hypocrite.

Unbreakable

Ms Gaga,

I am responding to your open letter to my daughter Kelly, and I am perplexed as to why you would go public with an open letter. Regarding this current situation: Kelly didn't contact you, I was the one that contacted your manager today and the email is attached below for your reference. I reached out to him as Kelly's manager and mother to ask him if you could address your 'little monster' fans and stop them from writing libellous, slanderous and vile comments about my family, including death threats to Kelly. Your open letter is hypocritical and full of contradictions. And as your mother Cynthia supports you, I support my daughter Kelly. I must say, your opinions on what is politically correct and acceptable totally differ from mine, but that is what makes the world so interesting . . . we are all different. How sweet that you have empathy for my daughter, as you feel that she has taken a less compassionate path in life. You say her work on E! with the *Fashion Police* is 'rooted in criticism, judgment, and rating people's beauty against one another'. Welcome to the real world. Example, when I saw you wear a dress made out of raw meat, I was sickened. When I see you wearing fur, and using it as a fashion statement, the fact that defenceless animals have been killed so you can get your picture in the press is abhorrent to me. Shouldn't you be teaching your 'little monster' fans to respect animals, and life? I don't feel I have to justify Kelly's choices in life to you. By your actions to Kelly right now, you have shown me that you are nothing more than a publicity-seeking hypocrite and an attention seeker. You know it would have been much more dignified of you to do this privately. I am calling you a bully because you have 32 million followers hanging on your every word and you are criticising Kelly in your open letter. Are you so desperate that you needed to make this public?

You state: 'Every day, through my music and public voice, I choose to be positive and work towards a kinder and braver world with our community of followers.' This is obviously not translating well to your fans, as a large portion of them have not only been vile to Kelly, but also to other celebrities such as

Madonna, Adele and Rihanna. You say 'a kinder and braver world'. I don't know what world you live in, but supporting disgraceful fan comments doesn't fall under the words 'kinder and braver'. It comes under the heading of bullshit.

In closing, stop wearing fur, stop looking for publicity and stop using your fans to belittle not just Kelly but an endless stream of celebrities. A word from you would stop all the hideous, negative and vile threats from your 'little monsters'. Let me know if you want to continue this debate. I'm an open playing field for you, my darling.

Sincerely,

Sharon Osbourne

As far as I am concerned, everything that Gaga is trying to stop – i.e., bullying – she's perpetuating by not telling her fans to do the same. That's the responsibility. If you're an artist, and your followers are threatening other people, you can't just give them free rein. That's insane behaviour, especially for the times that we live in when kids are going to school and fucking mowing down their classmates.

By not repudiating her fans' bullying behaviour towards Kelly and others, she was condoning it. And that's why I called her a hypocrite.

I was so disappointed with her attitude because I had always been a huge fan. I have been to three of her shows and she's undeniably a very talented woman. But you can't bang on about being anti-bullying and then refuse to tell your fans directly to stop haranguing other young women with nasty threats.

On Gaga's last tour, there would be a bus parked out front of each venue and she put therapists in there, for kids who were unhappy or being bullied. It's all well and good for a vulnerable young person to go and have fifteen minutes or half an hour's chat with a therapist, but where's the follow-up? I felt it was just a publicity stunt.

Perhaps the next time she has one of these mobile counselling stations, she should go in and ask the therapist for advice on setting good examples for her fans.

6

Talking with Friends

Comparing diamonds with Joan Collins on *The Talk*.

Anyone who was a fan of the ground-breaking US comedy series *Roseanne* will remember Roseanne's deeply sarcastic daughter, Darlene. She was played by a very talented actress called Sara Gilbert, who I first met when she came to a book-signing of *The Osbournes* in 2002, specifically to meet us. She was really lovely and very straightforward, just the kind of person I get along with. So, years later, when she called me to ask if I was interested in doing the pilot for a new show she'd come up with, I said yes immediately.

The concept was a simple one: a panel of five women of different ages, all with children, filtering the day's stories or issues through a mother's eyes – a similar idea to *Loose Women* in the UK. Barbara Walters has hosted a hugely successful show on ABC called *The View*, which has been running for seventeen years. But we weren't in competition. *The Talk* is much less political. Sara had originally come up with the idea because, when she was pregnant, she joined a mothers' group which got together each week and would discuss whatever issues arose around raising kids and families generally. There are no qualifications for mothering, and most of us come to it completely cold, inexperienced and unprepared. In these days of nuclear families, few of us have access to a network of aunts and grandmothers who, in earlier generations, would have been the main source of advice. Sara said she had found these sessions really interesting and helpful. The show would just be a bigger version of the same thing.

The ethos was very much focused around the five women talking in an organic, natural way about ordinary things that affected us all as parents. Having seen *The Osbournes*, Sara naturally felt I might have the right experience to bring to the table. And of the five proposed panellists, I was the only one with older children.

The other women's children ranged from one year to age fourteen. The show hadn't been commissioned at this point; it was just a pilot for CBS. If they liked it, they would take it. If they didn't, it would end up in that same toilet where five episodes of *Osbournes Reloaded* were blocking the U-bend.

The original line-up was Sara, me, news anchor Julie Chen, whose husband is CEO of the network, actress Holly Robinson Peete who I had done *Celebrity Apprentice* with, and *The King of Queens* actress Leah Remini.

Although the show got commissioned, the first season felt really uncomfortable. It just didn't gel. Backstage, everyone was arguing constantly, unable to agree on the topics for discussion, and it felt like everyone was jockeying for position. Who was going to be the funniest? Who was going to do the craziest thing? Who could shout everyone else down? Yuck.

I had really been looking forward to working on *The Talk* because I imagined it would be a friendly, fun thing to do. How wrong you can be. I remember sitting in the morning meetings, thinking, Fucking hell, what's going on? It wasn't what I expected at all. I got on well with Sara, and Julie was a real pro. She had done CBS news for sixteen years in New York, and she also hosts *Big Brother*. But Holly and Leah were another matter.

Our day would start at 8 a.m. with a morning meeting, to chat through potential topics with the producer. It proved surprisingly hard to find issues to fit with the mothering format. We would all chip in with various thoughts, give our slant on whether we were for or against a point of view, then head off back to our respective dressing rooms to get the warpaint on.

We would have a second meeting at 10.15 a.m. to finalise the content, before going live at 11 a.m., and always either Holly or Leah would never seem happy with what had been chosen.

Holly had been in two hit sitcoms, one in the eighties and one in the nineties. She was an actress who wasn't used to working without a script, so it was difficult for her. Unless you're an over-the-top personality, or a writer, or a stand-up comedienne, it's extremely hard to be engaging and witty on tap five days a week, particularly on live TV. Holly is mother to four gorgeous children, and in addition she is a philanthropist who's done great things for Parkinson's disease and autism. She works tirelessly for her causes. But I never felt she was at ease in this situation, though we never spoke about it.

As for Leah, she was a strange one. A very tough lady; a Scientologist. And that was the elephant in the room. Everybody knew, but it was never discussed. I honestly don't know what the fuck Scientology is. Is it a religion? A philosophy for life? I know it's got something to do with spaceships. The truth is, I didn't give a fuck what she believed in. It was none of my business. Whatever turns you on. I've heard that she's since left them. But at the time it was like a secret sect that the rest of us were excluded from. Leah's crassness intimidated everyone around her – particularly the crew. I understood that for Leah, as for Holly, this show was a different animal because she usually worked with scripts. In my experience the majority of actresses – and actors, there's nothing gender-specific in this – are so used to playing roles that they find it hard just to be 'themselves'. And that's what was needed on our show. The irony was that *The Talk* was supposed to be about celebrating women – their differences, their warmth, their spontaneity. I never found Leah to be either warm or cuddly, and certainly not the kind of woman you'd feel comfortable telling your innermost secrets to.

Women are often portrayed very badly on American television, particularly in those 'housewife'-style reality shows where everyone is fighting and back-stabbing. On air, we were the antithesis of that, but it would have been nice if we'd replicated that off air, too. Unfortunately, it rarely felt that way. Sisterhood, I'm afraid, had packed her bags and left the building.

At the end of the first season, we were on hiatus for five weeks when I got a phone call from one of the team to say that Leah and Holly's options had not been picked up.

We were told that it was 'a creative decision', that the bosses felt the vital chemistry they place so much emphasis on in the world of TV just wasn't there. The network doesn't get involved in who doesn't like who behind the scenes; the executives would just go on what came across on screen and the results of any audience research. If you don't get on in *front* of that camera, you can't wing it.

When I went back after the break, I was apprehensive. I wasn't sure if there was still going to be bad feeling, and, if there was, I didn't know if I could take it. Everyone wants to spend their day in a job that's enjoyable, where you all get on. Was that too much to ask?

I needn't have worried. Two new women had been brought in as replacements for Holly and Leah, comedienne Sheryl Underwood and actress and stand-up comic Aisha Tyler, and right from day one they were amazing. We all clicked in an instant and, from then on, it has become the best TV job I have ever had.

But, of course, as has happened so many times in my life, just as things were looking up, something jumped up and bit me.

When one of her Twitter followers asked Leah why she was no longer on the show, she tweeted back, 'Sharon. She had us fired.' She followed it up with, 'Sharon thought me and Holly were "Ghetto" [her words], we were not funny, awkward and didn't know ourselves.' She was referring to an interview I had given to the famously outrageous radio host Howard Stern, where I had said that to be successful on the show you had to know who you were, and that Holly and Leah clearly didn't.

I tweeted back: 'Leah knows that I have never been in a position to hire or fire anyone on the show. That being said, my only wish is that Leah would just stop all this negative, unprofessional and childish behaviour.'

Much as I would like to say that I am that powerful, I'm clearly not. I have trouble getting myself hired most of the time, so how the fuck could I get someone fired? I learned the lesson the hard way while working on *The X Factor* that in a 'she goes or I go' situation, the answer was . . . I was not on the next series of *X Factor*. Lesson learned.

Regardless, I was the bad guy, apparently. But really it was just an excuse. No one in TV wants to say their options weren't picked up because they didn't come out well in audience research, do they? They wanted a scapegoat. But, seriously? If I had that much fucking clout at CBS, I'd have my own bloody talk show!

In public, Holly maintained a dignified silence about Leah's claims, but she sent me a couple of unpleasant emails, making her feelings very clear indeed. Also, her mother wrote to my make-up artist, Jude Alcala, who has been with me for thirteen years, saying that he should know that he worked for an 'evil' person.

Obviously he showed me what she wrote, and while it's not pleasant being referred to in those terms, it didn't upset me one jot because I didn't even know the woman. What I felt was anger that she had involved poor Jude. What the hell did she think *he* was going to do about it?

So I called her straight away.

'Hey, missus, call or write to *me*, you know where I am. You live down the road from the studio, you could have come in to see me.'

I said that Jude had been with me for a long time and that she shouldn't place him in that awkward position; that she had made herself look like a fool.

'Right, so now we're on the phone to each other, tell me what your problem is.'

She started off with the whole 'you got my daughter fired' nonsense, and said that when she went into her local grocery store, everyone was telling her how much they missed having Holly on the show. That's just great, I said, but seriously, it has nothing to do with me.

In many ways, my heart went out to this woman. I understood why she had done it. She was a mother defending her daughter, just as I would do with mine.

But it was based on a lie, and I wasn't going to take it lying down just to make her feel better.

So I told her that she only had her daughter's side of the story, that TV was a tough game and that Holly probably hadn't researched well, which is why she wasn't picked up. I pointed out that all these shows do market research and that you can be the bitch from hell but if you come across well on screen, it will keep you in a job. That's all it comes down to, I said. Nothing more sinister than that. I wasn't going to be anyone's scapegoat.

It was Sara's show; she was the producer. Julie is married to the boss of the network. And Holly and Leah thought it was little old me that got them fired? I was just a hired hand with a big mouth. Don't pick on *me*, ladies.

For season two, the premise of the show changed. We were still five mothers, but we could talk about whatever we wanted. That was manna from heaven for me, with one small problem. It's live, and I sometimes forget myself. As we all get on so well, it's easy to think I'm sitting round a dinner table and chatting to my mates.

And in situations like that, we sometimes say things we think are funny, but which we don't really mean.

Luckily, given my propensity to swear, we are on a seven-second delay and have the lovely Kingsley, whose job it is to hit the big red cut-out button every time one of us – admittedly, mostly me – lets a rude word slip out. Kingsley is English and has a great sense of humour, so I walk past him each morning and say, 'Fuck, shit, fart,' to get it out of the way, and he raises his eyes heavenward at my naughtiness.

But Kingsley's job is only to hit that button for swear words. After that, we're on our own, and one or two of my off-the-cuff quips that *I* thought were funny at the time have got me into trouble afterwards. It's usually something glib that just pops into my head, and when I analyse it the next day, I think, Why did I say that? It's about finding that balance between speaking your mind, even if your view is controversial, and saying it in a way that isn't offensive to viewers.

In July 2011, a Californian woman called Catherine Kieu cut off her estranged husband's penis and threw it in the waste-disposal unit because he had reportedly started seeing an ex-girlfriend.

Before I knew it, I had opened my mouth and uttered the words, 'I don't know the circumstances . . . However, I do think it's quite fabulous.'

Obviously, I don't think it's fabulous at all and, to this day, I don't know what possessed me to say it. It just popped out. Luckily, Sara counteracted it slightly by saying that it was sexist to joke about it because if it was a woman's breast that had been cut off, we wouldn't be making light of it. Quite right – I was completely in the wrong.

But the damage was already done. By the time we came off air, the 'indignant viewer' emails had started pouring in. Some of them were absolutely furious. It had been such a knee-jerk comment, I didn't really think anyone would take it that seriously. Little did I know quite *how* serious it was yet to get.

A couple of days later, a message came in from some men's group saying that I needed a bullet to the back of my head, and suddenly the production team were having crisis meetings. CBS were fantastically supportive and put on extra-tight security for the following two weeks. The threats didn't keep me awake at night, but I'd be lying if I said they didn't unnerve me a little, because there's always one nutter, isn't there? It only takes one.

I had been planning to address the issue again on air, but after all the backlash, and receiving a death threat, I said diddly-squat about it. It was like, *what* penis remark?

That's what I find so hard about all this new technology now. There is always someone, somewhere who takes offence, and all they have to do is write a quick email and push the 'send' button. In the old days, when you had to write out a letter of complaint by hand, stick it in an envelope and wander off to the postbox, you *really* had to care about the point you wanted to make.

After the Catherine Kieu incident, I half expected to be given a talking-to by someone from the network or production team, but it didn't come. They were really good about it. They're the number-one network in America and have been for sixteen years. It's a huge corporation, yet it's like a family. They care about people.

But I'm a realist. I'm employed to do a job, so if it's not right for their network and I am going to get them in trouble by expressing a certain viewpoint, then of course they'll say something. They tell me all the time, 'OK, you've taken it too far, don't do that, it's not right for our viewers.' They know better than me, and I damn well listen. I'd be stupid not to. Again, it's that fine line between not being too outrageous, but not ending up with five co-hosts all sitting there too terrified to open their mouths in case it upsets one woman in Baltimore.

Last summer, we had a woman called Rielle Hunter on as a guest. She had written a 'spiritual' book about her affair with married Republican senator John Edwards, whose wife Elizabeth had had breast cancer and has since died. She had been unkind about Elizabeth in the book, which I thought was beyond inappropriate. It was disgusting. To my mind, she pursued him and was no better than a political groupie. She waited for him outside a hotel then gave her phone number to his assistant, for God's sake. Very unlikeable behaviour. So there she was, telling her story, and I just thought she wasn't being honest, and said so.

'Do you talk with forked tongue? That's what I want to know, Rielle.'

She started to cry, but honestly – what did she

expect? If you're going to come on a show with five other women and tell us about your affair with the husband of a woman with four kids who is dying of cancer, well, sorry, missy, you're going to get some stick. There was no way I was going to sit there and be false. If you're going to write a book about having an affair, own it. Say that you know it's not right and that he probably fed you a load of old lies about his wife, as they always do. But don't sit there and try to justify it.

After the show, the feedback revealed that most of the viewers agreed with me, and the show's bosses were obviously OK with it too, because I didn't get told off!

But it's a paradox; what I love about the show – that we are all mates and comfortable with each other – can also be my undoing, because I sometimes forget that there are people at home listening to our every word.

For me, *The Talk* has been like finding a home. I feel I belong. And I feel accepted. It's grounded me. Of course I still get great satisfaction out of working in the music industry, but only so far as the projects involve my husband. For everything else, I've seen it all before a million times. I've worked with some of the most legendary artists in the business. But if it wasn't for Ozzy, I could quite happily close the door and wave it all goodbye.

After all my TV endeavours, I have finally found somewhere I feel truly comfortable. Julie Chen is a self-made woman who has learnt her craft of journalism the hard way. I've watched her blossom into the hilariously funny, sexy presenter that she is today. She's the glue that holds the show together, the quintessential profes-sional. Off camera she's as funny as fuck, and I trust her implicitly.

As for Sara Gilbert, my darling little lesbian who first had the courage to hire me, she reminds me of a baby bird in a nest and I always want to protect her. She's wickedly funny and has a very naughty, dirty sense of humour and amazing comic timing. She became a star at a very early age, but through it all she has managed to stay grounded and is probably one of the wisest women I have ever known. I admire her immensely, as she came out openly on the show, which can't have been easy. She has two beautiful young children and she talks honestly about her sexual orientation, and in doing so

I know that she's helped thousands of young people feel comfortable with who they are. Also, for a working actress to come out in such a public way is taking a huge risk because it could easily affect a career. There are some pretty small-minded people out there, even in showbiz.

The first time I was introduced to Sheryl Underwood, Julie Chen called and asked me to join her and Sheryl for a breakfast meeting at the Beverly Hills Hotel Polo Lounge. This was after Holly and Leah's options hadn't been renewed and she had told me that CBS were thinking of adding Sheryl to the show. Sheryl is a stand-up comic, but back then I had no idea who she was, any more than she knew who I was.

The morning of the meeting, I woke up not feeling my usual self. I had a headache and felt extremely hot. As usual, I arrived at the meeting ten minutes late. We were seated in a booth and I was in the middle, with Sheryl on my left and Julie on my right. We ordered breakfast and proceeded to discuss the show. Julie knew Sheryl of old and was well versed in her history, so she introduced us, ate and ran. We must have been at least forty-five minutes into our meeting when I felt something was wrong. I had a sweaty top lip, my armpits were tingling and my stomach was definitely not right. I realised that I was missing half of what Sheryl was saying.

Sitting at the table opposite were Nicole Ritchie, her husband and her two lovely children. I've known Nicole for the last twelve years, so we'd already acknowledged each other and thrown air kisses in the way you do. I had just made eye contact with Nicole's husband when my mouth opened and I projectile-vomited. Fortunately the cascade of sick didn't reach him, but it did reach Sheryl, exploding over the both of us and our breakfasts. As introductions go, it could have been better.

Hastily excusing myself, I ran to my Range Rover and headed straight to my apartment, which was five minutes' drive from the hotel. But before I got there I shat myself all over the ivory-coloured leather seats. There are never fewer than three doormen to greet you at my apartment block and there's also a concierge behind the reception desk. My dilemma was this: how the fuck do I get into the building? I was covered in puke and shit, and the smell in the car was making me want to throw up again. So I called up to my house-keeper, Saba, who brought down bin bags, wet towels and a dressing gown. In the meantime, I parked in a side street until she arrived to clean me up.

So it wasn't the *greatest* introduction of all time . . . But Sheryl happens to be one of the funniest women I have ever met in my life and she took it all in her stride. I absolutely adore her, and subsequently I considered her my new bestie. She's always got my back.

The other new lady on *The Talk* was Aisha Tyler. She is a multitalented actress/stand-up comedienne/writer, and I've known her for eleven years. I interviewed her at least three times on my chat show in 2003. She's got that lethal combination of beauty and wit and is a complete workaholic – her résumé is endless. I'm in awe of her.

When Kelly came on *The Talk* as a guest, she made a point of thanking my four co-hosts on air for being so supportive. 'My mum doesn't have many female friends,' she said. 'So it's nice that she now has you guys in her life. She loves you all very much.'

She's right on both counts. It's true that I don't have a massive group of friends of either sex. But those I do have are very close indeed. And as I have always told my kids, it's not the number of friends you have, it's the quality. At the darkest times of my life, they have always been there for me. I can count them on both hands and, without exception, we have all grown up together.

My best friend is Gloria Butler, who is married to Geezer, Black Sabbath's bassist. She's about the only person in the world who still calls him Terry, apart from me when I'm talking to her. We first met when they were just dating and we've been friends ever since, even through the various ups and downs of Sabbath. She's four years younger than me and lives around the corner from us in Beverly Hills. We speak every single day without fail, and if she's walking her dogs past the house, she'll always pop in. She's very funny, and so like me in that she manages her husband and is very protective of him. She's American, from St Louis, Missouri and Geezer is from Birmingham, so there's quite a cultural difference, but it works.

I ring her on my way to work at about 7.15 a.m. and we talk for the duration of the drive to the studio, which is about fifteen minutes. She has two boys: the eldest is married with kids, just like Jack, and the other is Kelly's age. Incredibly, we had them three weeks apart, so the kids pretty much grew up together. We have so much shared history it makes friendship a lot easier because we don't have to go over old ground every time we speak. You can just have one of those quick, 'Hi, how are you' chats rather than spending the first ten minutes bringing someone up to date on your entire life.

Another really close friend is Belle Zwerdling, who I met in 1976 when I moved to Los Angeles at the tender age of twenty-four. She was my first American friend and we've stayed close ever since. Belle is now a very well respected Hollywood agent and a big part of who I am.

Before Ozzy and I started our romance, and it was just a working relationship, I even hooked him up with Belle. He was very lonely and needed female company, if you know what I mean, and Belle was well up for it. Both of them claim they never 'did the deed' as they were too busy telling jokes and laughing. According to Ozzy, Belle 'would sit on top of my bed with her legs crossed and she spent the entire time eating pickles'. After their first date – if that's what you could call it – Belle left Ozzy's hotel room wearing his jacket – a nice green and white check – and in the inner pocket was Ozzy's return ticket to London together with his passport. It was only a couple of months later when he needed it that Ozzy told me where it was. So I called her.

'Listen, Belle. Ozzy needs his ticket and passport and they're in that jacket you took. I need them back.' Her response was short and to the point: 'Ticket and passport yes, jacket no.'

Then there's Michele Anthony, who I've known for thirty years. Our lives run strangely parallel in that her father, Dee Anthony, was the US equivalent of my father. The difference is that she chose education and I didn't. She's a lawyer and was at Sony Music for eighteen and a half years and ended up running the company. After leaving Sony – which was Ozzy's label – she set up her own marketing consultancy and now has the luxury of working only with artists who are friends of hers. When I was working on the recent Black Sabbath album, Michele was the first person I turned to. We would never have got a number-one album without her. One of the gifts of getting to our age is that I trust her, and she trusts me, with everything. And we're talking here about multimillion-dollar deals, other people's careers. She's so wise that she's the person I go to for advice every time I need it. She lives in New York, so whenever I'm there we do our best to meet up. We can go for weeks without talking to each other, but we never have to explain why we haven't been in touch. We simply pick up where we left off. That's true friendship.

And along with my three girlfriends there's Colin Newman. Colin and I met when I was about eighteen and he was twenty-three and he worked for my father's accountant as a bookkeeper. Subsequently he passed his accountancy exams with honours and ended up buying the business. He and I became instant friends, although I used to drive him nuts whenever I went into the office. I'd fuck around with all his paperwork, scribble on everything I could see, go through his clients' accounts when he wasn't looking and basically cause uproar and mayhem. When I moved to Los Angeles in 1976, he would regularly come over on business trips for my father so we were always in touch. In fact, one time I even tried to fix him up with Belle too . . . ! I guess my matchmaking skills aren't up to much. Anyway, nothing came of it, as he married his then receptionist, the lovely Danish beauty Mette. As a result, our three lives have been constantly intertwined since our early twenties. It was a total coincidence that Colin handled Black Sabbath in those early days, and Ozzy has known him as long as I have. He's now our business manager, mine and Ozzy's – a *consigliere* to us both. Mette and Colin have four great children who were brought up with our three: their daughter Fleur – Kelly's best friend – now works in the music industry and I'm always consulting her, soliciting her opinion on all the new upcoming bands. So Ozzy, Colin, Michele, Belle, Gloria and me, we all connect.

And finally, one of the friendships I value most of all is the one I share with Elton John and David Furnish. I've known them both for years – particularly Elton who I met way back when we were both just kids starting out. Whenever I have needed him, he's been there for me and for my children too. This year he performed at the Nancy Davis 'Race to Erase MS' event where Jack was being honoured. He was meant to perform three songs but instead, Elton being Elton, he performed for over an hour.

I think we all have special people like this in our

lives – if we're lucky. Relationships that have stayed the distance until you're more than just friends – there's a bond you build up over years. You can go for ages without speaking and click together again in an instant. That's a connection worth more than all the money in the world and it becomes more and more important as the years go by.

And in the tough times ahead, when I thought I couldn't go on, it was these friends who helped pull me through. Thank God for them.

7

Back on Top

Back at number 1, where he belongs.

In early 2010, we restarted discussions about an album and reunion tour with all the original members of Black Sabbath. Right from the start, Ozzy had reservations about it because he'd been calling the shots for so long, doing his own thing. He'd always stayed close to Bill and Geezer, so any misgivings weren't on the personal front. It was more to do with business because, of course, everyone works differently.

'I'm worried about all the old baggage,' he told me over supper in our kitchen at Hidden Hills one night. There were four big egos involved here, and all of them deservedly so.

Initially I had come up with a three-year plan for

Sabbath which included writing, recording and touring – a huge commitment, given the age they all were. Three years is a long time when you're in your sixties. Precious time. Time not to be wasted. As for the proposed album, they had tried to write one years before and it hadn't worked. Now Ozzy was scared that if they attempted it again, it would be the same old story: a huge chunk out of his life that he couldn't get back again.

He was always saying, 'If the album's shit, is it going to be all my fault?' It was a rhetorical question; he wasn't expecting me to have an answer.

He absolutely wanted to do it, but when he wrote down on a pad the pros and the cons, the cons column was considerably longer than the pros. It meant giving up his own successful band, his bandmates, his commitment to Sony Records – there were still three albums to deliver; not options, these were firm. It meant giving up his own publishing. The list went on. In the end, what persuaded him to go for it was that the legendary record producer Rick Rubin had agreed to work with them on it. Rick is phenomenal. He helped popularise hip hop, and MTV recently named him 'the most important producer of the last twenty years'. He is a music guru who can work with any genre. And a producer who can have a hit album with Metallica, Johnny Cash, Neil Diamond, Adele and then Black Sabbath has got to be something. He is a musical genius.

He was so good with Sabbath because he knew how to treat them, how to bring out the best in their performance. He nurtured them, he told them constantly, 'You *can* do this.' They had never really had that kind of encouragement before.

Something else that was new to them was that he had balls and wasn't afraid to speak his mind. Rick Rubin wasn't a yes-man. He was quite capable of telling them, 'I don't like that song, actually. It's not going to go on the album.' No one had ever said that to them before, so they were in shock. But without Rick on board, pushing them, they would have been far more easily satisfied. Old habits die hard, and they would have written ten songs, then said, 'OK, here's the album – put it out.' And no one would have questioned that – not me, not anyone. But Rick did; he made them keep working at it. He had a clever way of dealing with their egos, of getting them to go that extra mile. He would tell them that their songs were really good, but that he knew they could still do better. They were pushed, really pushed, steadily but so gently that they barely noticed what was happening. He never raised his voice. He just has this uncanny gift of going into their minds, into their psyches. Put simply, he knows how to get the best from musicians.

They made the reunion announcement on 11 November 2011 at Hollywood's Whisky A Go Go club, on Sunset Boulevard, which had been their first LA gig ever in 1970. So this was a part of Sabbath's history, and the first time all four of them had been pictured together since their induction into the US Hall of Fame in 2006. The news was well received by the industry. *Kerrang!* said, 'They are the Beatles of heavy metal. It all starts with Black Sabbath.'

It was all very upbeat and exciting, but behind the scenes there were a few issues. As fucking ever.

Bill, the drummer, had been suffering from heart problems, but everyone was adamant that he come on board with the album and the tour, and he agreed, but negotiations were long and complicated and lawyers' bills went through the roof.

In the meantime, the writing sessions with Tony,

Ozzy and Geezer continued and, in October 2012, Tony was in New York to promote his autobiography, *Iron Man*, before flying on to LA and coming to Ozzy's studio at our house in Hidden Hills. But each day he kept saying he didn't feel well, and it was clear to me that he wasn't his old self. Tony Iommi is a big man, but he looked diminished somehow, sallow and much quieter than usual. Ozzy urged him to see a doctor in LA, but he refused. He would see his own doctor when he got back to England, he said. And he did, when he went home for Christmas, when he was diagnosed with the early stages of lymphoma. He started treatment immediately.

When Ozzy heard the news, he went into deep shock. This was someone he'd grown up with, someone he'd known his entire life, so inevitably it made him look at his own mortality. For Ozzy, Tony *was* 'the iron man', and when someone he perceived as so strong was floored by cancer, it devastated him.

Naturally, Tony could no longer make the journeys to LA because of his condition and ongoing treatment. In fact, we were all amazed when he said he was determined to continue with the album. So the plan changed.

Now all the writing would have to be done at Tony's home studio in Solihull just south of Birmingham. We established that it would be in sessions of five weeks, because on the sixth week Tony would go into hospital. Everything was changed, and rightly so, to accommodate Tony and the new situation.

Ozzy and Geezer would fly back and forth to Birmingham for these writing sessions. But when Ozzy was at home in Hidden Hills, he was hideous. I can't say it came as a surprise; he always is when he's writing an album, because he puts himself under enormous mental pressure, which makes him very hard to deal with – irritable and snappy. But this time he seemed even worse than usual. I put it down to the travelling, to the toing and froing between Birmingham and LA. My husband has never coped well with transatlantic travel, and now he seemed to be more asleep than awake. I assumed it was jet lag, as he always finds it hard for his body clock to adjust. But when he was awake, the least little thing I did would irritate him. I tried to be understanding. Tony had cancer. Ronnie Dio had just died of cancer. And they were all having to deal with this. They were having to go on not knowing what the future would hold. There was one good outcome: all the feuds, all the childish behaviour, all that love-you, hate-you stuff that had gone on for years was forgotten. None of this was important any more. In spite of all the bickering they had done in the past, ultimately these four guys had a love and a respect for each other. For Ozzy, 'iron man' Tony had always been a pillar of strength. All I could do was give him space.

As part of the marketing plan, Sabbath had been booked to do a headlining festival tour of Europe in the summer of 2012. It was the perfect vehicle to tease the album that was due for release in early 2013 by debuting a few of the new songs, and for the audience to see them all back together again. The tour dates had been finalised late in 2011, before anyone knew about Tony's health. His manager kept saying, 'He'll be all right. He's getting stronger.' After every treatment it would be, 'Just wait. Wait.' But I was worried. The dates were all sold out. And these are festivals, they're one-offs. They can't just be rescheduled – I mean, at each festival there may be fifteen other bands. So what do you do? You can't let down the fans, and you can't let down the promoters.

We agreed to monitor Tony's health and progression. Some months he was good, some months he wasn't. But the manager's line was always, 'Let's wait.' The issue wasn't the performing. It was the travelling; it was everything involved in getting him on that stage. We waited until the very last minute, but in the end it became clear that Tony just couldn't do it. He wanted to, but with the therapy he was having you're not supposed to fly because of the risk of picking up bacteria and viruses. So the decision was made that Ozzy would go out with his band, calling it Ozzy and Friends. And they were. He had Geezer and Slash and Zakk Wylde, and they all did a set. None of the new Sabbath songs were played, which was as it should be. Black Sabbath did appear that summer, but only in England. The first gig was at a small club venue in Birmingham on 19 May, in aid of Help for Heroes. The second was on 10 June, at the Download Festival at Donington Park in front of a crowd of 110,000. This was a spiritual experience because of Tony. Nobody knew if he was going to make it, but he had come back home in triumph. Everyone was chanting his name and it was magical.

After the tour was over, it was back to writing. In the end, they had thirty songs to choose from. The album was recorded in Malibu in Rick Rubin's studio, and Tony managed to get out for that. It was finally finished in January 2013.

Usually bands take one of the tracks as the album title, but this time nothing felt right and they called it *13*. The number thirteen has a multitude of meanings in different cultures, but it is always mystical. And so it would prove in this case. *13* went straight to number one in thirteen countries.

Once the album was finished and out there, all we could do was wait. Sabbath had always been the underdogs, the band that the majority of mainstream music journalists didn't understand. They were a blue-collar band with a blue-collar mentality and aggression. Their songs weren't about boy meets girl and walking in the sunshine. When a couple of the UK broadsheets slagged *13* off, I thought, Thank God, because if it had been well received by them it would have felt like the band had sold out.

Journalists are one thing, but the buying public is quite another. We all felt there was a huge hole in the marketplace for a great hard-edged rock album, but the question was, would Sabbath fill it?

When the pre-orders started to come in, we knew that it was going to be a number-one album in New Zealand, Denmark, Germany, UK, Scandinavia and Brazil. And then came the big one: America. After years and *years* of trying to get them acknowledged, not just for their body of work but for how they influenced other bands, they finally had their hard-earned validation. And as for Ozzy . . . well, I can't overstate what it meant to him. After all the borderline insane things he had done in his life, he had always said to me that he only had one ambition left: to get a number-one album in America. He had sold over 100 million albums worldwide as a solo artist and as a member of Black Sabbath, but he had never achieved that. And now he has, and he's done it with friends he has known since he was a teenager.

They are now, without question, the elder statesmen of what they do, much like Elton John, Rod Stewart or Paul McCartney. But of course, Ozzy's old insecurities are still there. Already he's saying, 'What happens now; how do we top that?'

Back on Top

But first there was the tour to get through. They toured Australia and Japan in the spring of 2013, and North America in the summer. South America came in October, finishing up on 22 December 2013 back in Birmingham, their home town, where it all started.

After this, the future is in their hands. At this point it's not even a discussion. All I know is that after forty-plus years of trailblazing music, good times, bad times, falling in and out of love with each other, they will go down in music history as the band that had a number-one album forty-three years into their career. No one else has come close. Their first album made number one in the UK on 1 January 1970, and it's still selling today. They will go down as one of the greatest, most innovative bands of all time.

8

Testing Times

The T-shirt says it all.

I t's fair to say that Ozzy's regard for his health has been limited to non-existent over the years, so we have often wondered what the future might hold for him. Then, in 2011, we got the chance to find out when a company called Knome got in touch to offer him a genome test.

In layman's terms, this 'determines likelihood of trait expression and disease risk' and, at the time, cost around $250,000 per person. But they said they would give it to us for free if they could publish Ozzy's results. It was a no-brainer because, given his very public, rather colourful life, he had nothing to hide, so we said yes immediately. Even better, they then offered it to me too.

They came to Welders, took three phials of blood from each of us and then we had to wait three months for the results. To be honest, I didn't give mine much thought during that time. My father had suffered from Alzheimer's, so I was interested in finding out the likelihood of my getting it too, but other than that, the focus was on Ozzy who, we assumed, would discover he'd done all manner of damage to himself with years of drink and drug abuse.

When the day came, a small silver box arrived with *Gnothi seauton* engraved on it: Greek for 'Know thyself'. Inside was a memory stick embedded in a foam casing, and on it were over three hundred test results. Thankfully there was an accompanying letter, because most of the medical data swam before my eyes. They also called us, just to flag up anything they felt might be of concern.

Astonishingly, Ozzy had fuck all to worry about. There was something about being allergic to dust, coffee and, surprise surprise, alcohol. But nothing serious at all. Then it came to my results.

I had two of the four genes that make you prone to Alzheimer's, which gave me a fifty-fifty chance of getting it. This was terrifying news for me because I had seen what it did to my father. It was a horrible way to go, something I wouldn't wish on anyone. But even though I couldn't do anything about it, I was glad that I knew, so that I could look for any telltale signs and prepare those around me as to how, *if* I got it, it might progress.

I forget things now. I can be halfway up the stairs and forget what on earth it was I was looking for, and I'm always losing my car keys. But this doesn't worry me because I know that everyone does things like that when they get older. I know Ozzy does. The crucial signs I will look out for are the things that happened to my father: forgetting the names of people really close to you, even those in your actual family, and having small panic attacks because certain images and words are just flashing in and out of your brain.

My father would have terrible anxiety attacks, but I don't know exactly when they started because, for so many years, we were estranged. I only came back into his life after he'd been diagnosed, and by that time he would only ever talk in short sentences, nothing in-depth. So I don't know how many of the

Alzheimer's genes he had, or when the disease first started to take hold. All I know is that I have a higher chance than most of getting it.

Meanwhile, I had another serious issue to think about. The test showed that I had the gene for colon cancer, which I already knew, but it also said that I had one of the specific faulty genes linked to breast cancer.

Great. So my husband, who had caned his body all his life with God knows what substances, was probably going to get a telegram from the Queen one day, and *I* was the one with the health problems. I think that's what they call Sod's Law.

According to the NHS, in the UK a woman's lifetime risk of developing breast cancer is ten per cent. Out of every hundred women, ten will develop breast cancer by the time they are eighty years old. It can affect anyone, even if they don't have a faulty gene. Having a fault in one of the breast-cancer genes, as I did, raises the risk of developing breast cancer to between fifty and eighty-five per cent.

Just before getting this news, one of my breast implants had been driving me insane. I'd had them put in about three years before and they had never felt right.

Now one was a completely different shape to the other, and it was drooping significantly. They were both bigger than I had ever wanted them, anyway, and I felt as if I had a waterbed on my chest. Be warned, all of you who think that implants will give you firm, perfect breasts for ever. They drop, just like breasts do anyway, but they drop even faster because of the weight. Few surgeons will tell you that.

As well as the right breast drooping, it was also getting really itchy underneath, right down to my ribcage. It would itch and itch all bloody day long. I just assumed it was eczema, even though I have never in my life suffered from it.

After getting the genome result, I went to see a breast-cancer specialist and also mentioned the itching. After studying my breasts, she said that she could tell something wasn't quite right, that perhaps the right implant was leaking. A mammogram and ultrasound scan confirmed her diagnosis, showing a grey patch spreading from my breast down to my ribcage. There was a strong chance that, if it wasn't dealt with, it could become infected.

It was a huge lesson to me. You think you can get

away with mucking about with your body, searching for the perfect breasts . . . it's always the breasts with us women, isn't it? I did it my whole life out of vanity, and now I was learning that there's a price for everything. The faulty gene is something you're either born with or not, but the leak was my doing because I chose to have silicone implants. I started to look back over all the surgeries I'd had out of vanity and thought, What the fuck am I doing?

I had three options: leave things as they were for a while, then return every six months for a mammogram to see if there had been any changes; go in for surgery and just remove the implants; or go in for surgery and have the implants *and* my breast tissue removed and be done with it.

I didn't think twice about it. I had three kids, and my first grandchild was on the way. For me, the double mastectomy was a very simple decision to make. They were coming off. My breasts had always been problematic for me because I was large-chested and they got on my nerves. The surgery had been about trying to reduce them, firm them up or stop them sagging, never about making them bigger. I didn't want to go back every six months for tests, and there was absolutely no point get-ting new implants put in when I might end up having to take them out again for a mastectomy further down the line. So I said to myself, Fuck it, I don't want to finish up looking like a patchwork quilt, I want them gone. I didn't want that time bomb inside me. I didn't feel the need to discuss it with anyone; it was totally my choice and I made it there and then.

When I got home and called the kids, they didn't want me to do it straight away, they wanted me to think about it. And Ozzy didn't really understand my reasons for doing it either. They were all pretty freaked out by it, to be honest. But when I made it clear that I was fine with it psychologically and that it was a preventative measure that meant I was less at risk, they were fully supportive.

Initially it was going to be two separate surgeries: six hours for the first, where they remove the implants and breast tissue, then, a few months later after you've healed, there's a seven-hour procedure for the aesthetic side of things.

But the first operation, in January 2012 at St John's hospital in Santa Monica, took thirteen and a half hours.

It turned out that the silicone had leaked into my stomach wall, and it took the surgeon all that time to pick it out. Hours and hours to sort out the mess. And for what? My fucking vanity. I am so against silicone breast implants now, and would urge any woman not to have them. They're revolting.

Then, after the stomach wall had been cleaned up, they put temporary, saline-filled implants in, just to stretch the skin.

Meanwhile, Kelly was at the hospital, anxiously waiting for me to emerge from surgery and fielding increasingly panicked calls from the others. So when, after six hours, there was no news, they started to think that something had gone terribly wrong and I wasn't coming back.

When I was finally brought up, so Kelly later told me, I was howling like a wounded animal; I have no recollection of this. Then I just cried and cried and cried, going on and on about my father or just talking complete gibberish. I think it was a reaction to the extra anaesthetic I'd needed to be kept under for longer. Either way, it was very scary and distressing for her.

I came out after five days, and was under strict

instructions to rest. As our house in Hidden Hills was quite a long drive and I couldn't face the journey, I took the decision to stay at our one-bedroom apartment in Sierra Towers, which we used for occasional overnights in LA if we were working there late. It was also several degrees cooler in town and, after the op, I was even more sensitive to heat than I usually am.

I have long had issues with excessive sweating, at night especially. It goes back to when I had the colon cancer and had to have chemo. They said my periods would probably stop, and I thought the sweating might be part of the menopause. But in the end, my periods carried on then petered out when I was about fifty-five.

I certainly wasn't aware of the menopause when, or indeed if, it came; I had no symptoms other than the sweating, which I still get. Sometimes I wake up in the morning with a lake on my chest, so I like to have the bedroom really cold, while Ozzy likes it to be warmer. I often think about crossing the hallway to the cooler spare bedroom, but rarely have the strength to do so.

So, post-mastectomy, I had a bed to myself at Sierra Towers and the air-con on full blast. But after the first day I fainted on my way to the bathroom. Luckily, as well as Ozzy, my housekeeper Saba was with me, thank God. She took me to Cedars-Sinai hospital, which was the nearest, where they ran some tests. It turned out that I had a critically low iron level, so I had to stay there for the next five days to get the level up, then return for weekly infusions until it had stabilised. The bag of iron was so thick that it took two to three hours to put in. You can't just do it through a syringe, and you have to get the proportions right or it can be dangerous.

Once I was home and healing, it still took me ages to get over the anaesthetic. I wasn't in any pain from the operation, as such, just discomfort. But I was so woozy. I would be fine in the morning, then about lunchtime I would start nodding off.

I took two weeks off straight after the operation, then went back to doing *The Talk*. I didn't say anything on air about the operation, but the girls all knew about it so they were able to keep an eye on me. They were so kind. Everyone rallied round to make sure I didn't get too tired.

After about three months, when everything from the first operation had settled down, I went in for the second, which took the expected time of seven hours.

Testing Times

First of all they removed the saline implants and fitted two nets inside my breasts. Then, while I was still under, they took body fat from my stomach area and put it into some sort of spinning machine. Usually if you inject fat into the body, it eventually dissipates, but apparently this spinning process helps it to stick to the netting. When I came round I was totally bandaged up, right across my chest, then fitted with a strong elastic bra with a zip up the front. I felt trussed up, but in a secure rather than uncomfortable way. After searching all my life for the 'perfect' breasts, I felt nothing but relief that they'd been removed. Not just because of the health issues, but because I just didn't have to think about them any more.

When Angelina Jolie had her double mastectomy, she made a point of saying that she didn't feel defeminised by it. That was an important thing to say, because I know that a lot of women do feel that way after the operation. But I didn't feel defeminised by it at all. I'm sixty, my kids are grown up and, for me, it just didn't feel like a big deal. But if someone like Angelina – in the prime of her life and such an exotic, mysterious, beautiful, physically *perfect* woman – can make such a huge decision and feel OK about it, that's a great message to put out there.

We're just lucky that medicine has come on in such leaps and bounds that we even *have* this preventative option. It wasn't that long ago that no one ever got an early warning; they only found out when it was too late.

When I had the colon cancer, it had gone into my lymph nodes. That is something I still have to keep an eye on because if it flares up again it can spread easily. So I go for a check-up once a year. I also check myself regularly for lumps, but other than that, I feel very calm about it all. I just get on with it. Ozzy gets more uptight about it than I do. He got to grips with all the medical detail in the end, but it only panicked him, so I steer away from in-depth conversations about it. Besides, I'm at an age now where I know what's best for me and I'm just going to do what I've got to do. My family can have a view if they wish, but ultimately it's my decision.

I think about all the women who aren't lucky enough to be in my position, who don't have the knowledge that the genes they're carrying might heighten their risk of getting breast cancer, and I consider myself to be very fortunate indeed. I have minimised the risk and I now have far smaller breasts made from my own body fat that feel much more comfortable. I barely even think about them now.

Once the scars from the second operation had healed, I went in and had a couple of nipples tattooed on, purely for aesthetic purposes. It was nothing, because I couldn't feel it being done anyway. It's something they encourage, just so that your new breasts resemble the old ones as much as they can. But to be honest, with or without nipples, when I looked in the mirror I was absolutely fine with what I had, and still am.

Now I sometimes go out in a dress or a kaftan and I don't wear a bra. It's so liberating, as I have never been able to do that before. Also, as I'm short, smaller breasts suit my shape much better. I wake up in the mornings and feel somehow lighter, unburdened by the thought of yet another mammogram looming and what they might find.

And, to boot, I have the most *fabulous* décolletage. Yes, dear reader, I confess. While I was under the anaesthetic for the second operation I figured that, as I was out for the count anyway, I might as well make the most of it. So while they were waiting for my body fat to spin in that wondrous little machine, I asked them to give me a cheeky little neck lift while they were at it. I always push it.

But not as much as my husband who, throughout all my time in hospital for these procedures, only came to see me once. And during that *one* visit he took a photograph of me, completely out of it, my face puffed up from the anaesthetic, my eyes like slits, my mouth dribbling. I didn't realise it had been taken until he sent it to me as a text message a few days after getting home. I was so upset about it that I went through the fucking roof.

'Why on earth would you do that? What's the fucking point you're trying to make?' I shouted.

'I just thought it was funny,' he said, and shrugged.

Not for the first time, I wondered if he knew me at all. Yes, I was angry, but actually, it broke my heart.

9

Pearly Princess

Look at that face!

After quite a few years of battling with substance abuse in his teens, my son Jack was finally in a really good place: clean and sober since the age of seventeen, super fit and gaining a reputation as quite a daredevil with TV shows like *Adrenaline Junkie*. His life was very much, 'Oh Mum, at the end of the month I'm off down the Amazon with some mates,' or, 'I'm going to climb a mountain, I'll be back in six weeks.' The mere thought of it gave me a heart attack each time, but I was thrilled that he had found something he loved doing and was really good at.

In April 2011, he started dating a girl called Lisa Stelly. I had met her a couple of times and really liked her. She was a working model, and had done TV commercials and was making a good living from it. She was a beautiful, long-legged young woman from Louisiana, with that lovely Southern accent, and it was no mystery to me what Jack saw in her. But it was very early days between them, so their relationship wasn't something I gave much thought to. Then, about three months after they met, Jack called me while I was staying a couple of nights in town.

'Mum, are you around? We need to talk.'

Now if this had come from Kelly, I would instantly go into mental free fall and think, What *has* she done now? But as Jack was so sensible, I imagined it was a business matter he wanted to discuss with me, or another madcap, dangerous adventure he was embarking on. So as he walked in the door, I had mentally prepared myself for all the nail-biting details.

'Hi, Mum. Now, look, don't panic and don't get upset . . .'

Which, of course, immediately made me panic. My heart was in my chest, my mind racing with all the possibilities of what he was about to tell me. Well, all except the *actual* one.

'Lisa's pregnant.'

A wave of different emotions washed over me. One of them, of course, was joy, because there was a new life coming into the world. But then I was sad too, because my son and his girlfriend barely knew each other, and I knew that from this moment on his life would never be the same again. All I could think of for a while was that I didn't know Lisa, and I just hoped she loved my son. You don't always know after two or three months, and I doubt she knew then either.

Ozzy was away on tour at the time, so I called to tell him. He never thinks of consequences, he just focuses on that one thing. So he says, 'A baby? That's amazing,' and meanwhile I'm sitting there thinking, Oh my God. What happens if it doesn't work, and one of them meets somebody they fall in love with and then gets married and goes?

Because as a mother, all these scenarios go through your head; you can't help it. But Jack's telling me, 'You can't think like that, Mum. You've just got to think about the positive.'

I had expected the first pregnancy to be one of my girls; I never expected it to be Jack, who is the baby of the family. And as he led such an active, outdoorsy sort of life, it just wasn't on the cards.

He was the first to acknowledge that he and Lisa were only just getting to know each other. But there was only ever one outcome. Lisa is very religious, and she's totally against abortion – as is Jack, though his views have nothing to do with religion. He just doesn't agree with it.

I really admired him for doing the right thing. There are so many guys who would have gone, 'Forget it; I'm off.' He didn't. He was responsible and supportive, and just amazing.

'All we can do,' he said, 'is try our hardest to make it work, and see if we can become a couple. We're not thinking about marriage yet; we're just thinking about the baby. So we've decided that Lisa's going to move in with me.'

Now Jack's house was a classic bachelor pad, up in the Hollywood Hills. There were about forty bloody steps up to it, and my first thought was, Well, *that's* going to be fun, carting a buggy up those.

So I knew straight away that we were going to have to sell the place, because it just wasn't child-friendly, but

I really admired them. It was such a grown-up approach to a difficult situation, and they are from totally different backgrounds and cultures. It was especially tough for her to say she was pregnant, coming from the very close-knit and religious Southern family she does. Her brother-in-law is a preacher.

Initially I supposed that I might not be as involved in the pregnancy as I would have been if it was, say, Aimee or Kelly who was having the baby, but Lisa was incredibly thoughtful towards me in everything. She let me be a part of all the ultrasound scans, which I thought was an amazing thing to do.

I would look at the jellybean on the screen, then across at my son. And suddenly I was rewinding a quarter of a century and it was me having the scan and looking at Jack on the screen. You don't realise how quickly time passes, and to me, it might have been yesterday that I had him. Then I would snap out of it and think, What *am* I doing? I'm insane.

It was so special to be there, watching my son's face as he saw his tiny daughter on the screen. He was just overwhelmed. Overwhelmed and overjoyed. And I was really happy to see that, because there were times when so many people – Jack's friends included – thought the whole thing was crazy, saying, 'It's never going to work,' and, 'You're nuts to even try,' and yet here they were, Jack and Lisa, two young people united in love for their unborn child.

Pearl entered our lives on 24 April 2012. It was a natural birth, with Lisa's mum in the delivery room with her, plus her sister who was videoing it, while Jack, Ozzy, Kelly and I were waiting outside in the hallway along with other members of Lisa's family.

Lisa had had a couple of false starts but when she was about ten days late, they decided to bring her in and induce her. When I heard the news, I remember becoming aware of my heart beating faster. My first grandchild. I took a few deep breaths and it was a case of, Right, this is it. Now. Nothing will ever be the same again. By the end of the day there'll be a baby. A new little Osbourne. And in the end, everything went perfectly. There was no panic, it was all very controlled and bonding. Exactly the way you would want it to be.

When Pearl was born, it was indescribably moving. Now I understand why people become midwives – the emotion, the wonder, the glory of it, is intoxicating. To be in the presence of something so extraordinary, to share this moment, this everyday miracle, was a privilege. I kept looking at Jack's face the whole time, and I could tell that he was trying as hard as I was to stay composed but, of course, he broke down and cried. We all did, but the two brand-new grandmothers out-sobbed everyone else.

The midwife swaddled the precious bundle in a blanket and we took turns cradling her as we welcomed this new addition to our two families. She was a complete amalgam of the two of them, with Jack's mouth and chin and Lisa's nose and eyes. I was so moved, and just couldn't stop the tears from cascading down my cheeks. With her wisp of pale brown hair, still damp from her momentous journey, she was just adorable and I was overwhelmed with love for her.

The joy on her parents' faces was plain for all to see, and I felt instinctively at that point that, despite the shock of the pregnancy so early in their relationship, they were going to do just fine.

I was still in a state of trance, talking to my co-grandmother Gerri, each of us trying to find the words to express our emotion, creating a bond between us that will last a lifetime. And then my phone rang.

It was Simon Cowell. Blimey, I thought, news travels fast. Pearl's only minutes out of the pod and already he's calling to congratulate me. In fact, I was particularly pleased when I saw his name flash up as, only the previous week, me and my big mouth had been making headlines with Simon as the focus, and I wasn't sure how he had taken it.

In his supposedly authorised biography *Sweet Revenge: The Intimate Life of Simon Cowell*, there was a random, throwaway sentence where Simon was quoted as saying that he didn't like working with me. No reason was given, no explanation, which made it even more baffling. I had always thought Simon and I had a good working relationship and made good television together, so I was hurt, really hurt. And when the subject of his remark was raised on *The Talk*, I said that he was clearly suffering from small penis syndrome. I don't know why I said it, beyond wanting to hurt him. Saying that he had a small dick was all I could think of that might upset him as much as he had upset me.

It was totally ridiculous. I have never seen Simon in

the altogether. I don't even know why I felt so hurt. Normally, if it isn't someone close, if I don't give a fuck about somebody, then I don't give a fuck what they think about me. But this felt different. Perhaps it was because I held him in such high esteem and have so much respect for what he's achieved that it hit me in the solar plexus. I had always enjoyed working with him, and his comment meant that the feeling wasn't reciprocated, which was humiliating.

However, what I said in return was obviously a joke. After all, how would a woman of my age in whom Simon had zero sexual interest know *what* size his bloody penis was? But of course the press seized on it and my flip comment got picked up worldwide.

Cut to one week later and there I was, a proud new grandmother, beaming from ear to ear and thrilled that Simon's call of congratulation meant that all was forgiven and forgotten. Water off a duck's back.

'Sharon, it's Simon. Why did you say that about me?'

Oh dear. He wasn't calling about the birth.

'Because you hurt *me* by saying you didn't like working with me.'

'I don't *want* to hurt you.'

'And I don't want to hurt *you*.'

'Good, so can we agree to stop it, then?'

'Absolutely.'

And that was it. We called a truce and made up. Then I told him about Pearl and he was genuinely delighted.

I think that Simon loves beautiful young women, which is totally normal, and he loves to be surrounded by them at all times. I don't fall into that category, so as he's a very busy man, and I'm a very busy woman, there has been no time for us really to get to know each other properly.

That's a shame, because I think we have the potential to be very good friends.

After the birth, Gerri stayed with Lisa and Jack for the first six weeks to help out. She and Lisa's father, Pat, live in New Iberia, Louisiana, midway between New Orleans and Houston, Texas. Whichever way you look, it's a long trek to California – they have to change planes twice. So I was glad that she was able to get some quality time with her new granddaughter before heading home.

By then, Jack and Lisa had moved from the place

with the forty steps to a lovely house in Los Feliz, Hollywood, which is a very young, creative, hipster district. Looking after a baby together is such a bond, and they are in no rush to get a nanny. They take care of Pearl themselves, and it's just lovely. Jack is very hands-on with everything and Lisa is such a confident, assured mother, despite it being her first time. She's made a wonderful home for Jack. She adores him and she's a fantastic mum. I couldn't ask for anything more for my son.

When Pearl was about a week old, Ozzy and I were over there visiting and we could tell there was something on their minds, but in a nice way.

'We've decided to get married,' said Jack, grinning with happiness. And it felt so natural, absolutely the right thing for them to do. They had barely known each other a year, but when you know, you know.

And what a year it had been. He'd had to move out of the bachelor pad he loved so much, his cherished bulldog Lola had died – a great character he'd had for thirteen years, since he was barely into his teens. And then he got appendicitis. He'd called me one evening saying he had a terrible stomach ache.

'Get Lisa to drive you to the hospital,' I told him. But she was very heavily pregnant, plus she was asleep. I couldn't help because I was miles away in Hidden Hills. He said he'd take himself to hospital. I told him to let me know when he got there. So he got himself to Cedars-Sinai and called me. They were admitting him for tests, he told me. 'But I'm fine.' This wasn't true. Unbeknown to me, they took him in and operated on him immediately. He told me later, but said that he hadn't wanted anyone to worry.

10

Stronger than Me

My brave boy Jack, with Pearl.

About two weeks after Pearl was born, Jack was doing a series for the Syfy channel on haunted houses, and it was quite an active job. For one of the shows, they lowered him into this lake in Utah where a body was supposed to be buried. So he had his air tanks on, and his suit, and he was going down in this lake, saying, 'Actually, this is *unbelievably* freezing.' He really felt it.

When he came out and was back at his hotel, he called me.

'I have the worst headache. I think it's a terrible migraine because the water was so cold.'

'Bloody hell, that doesn't sound good, Jack. Just go to bed and see how it is in the morning.'

When he woke up the next day, he called again.

'Mum, I can't see out of one of my eyes, and my head is still killing me.'

'You've got to see a doctor. Just get on a plane and come home.'

I knew straight away that this wasn't good. Two years earlier, when he was filming his dad's documentary, *God Bless Ozzy Osbourne*, and we were all on the road together, he kept saying, 'Mum, my leg feels weird all the way down to my feet – it's like pins and needles, but they're really hot.'

I told him then to see a doctor. I didn't want to worry him unnecessarily, but back in 1992 I'd done some research into multiple sclerosis when I thought Ozzy might have it. I had even joined a support group. And from what I remembered, what Jack was describing sounded suspiciously familiar.

'No, Mum. It's nothing serious. It's the L4, L5 area on my spine. It's my bad back, that's what's doing it. I'm going to go to my chiropractor.'

That's what he kept saying. Anyway, this went on for three months and he just learnt to live with it. He never did anything other than go and get his back cracked.

So when, two years later, he was talking to the doctor about the migraine and loss of sight, he mentioned the leg problem and, even though MS is very tricky to diagnose because there are so many symptoms, I think that was what pointed them in the right direction.

Jack went to see an eye specialist who said that, in his opinion, it was neurological. So next he went to the neurologist who said he needed an MRI scan. This time I went with him, and sat outside with the technician and his doctor.

I was sitting there, watching the images of Jack's brain as they popped up on the screen, and the technician pointed to an area showing a couple of white spots.

'See this?' he said. 'Looks like he may have had a stroke.'

He wasn't a doctor but, of course, these guys are overseeing scans all day long, so they pick things up along the way.

This scared the shit out of me because, until then, I had associated strokes with older people, not fit young men like Jack. But I did know that if you've had a couple of small, imperceptible strokes, it can mean that there's a much bigger, more damaging one on the way, particularly if, like Jack so often did in his work, you were doing something that involved a lot of physical exertion.

Jack's GP, who was sitting beside me, put a hand on my shoulder. 'Now hold on a minute. We don't know anything yet, Sharon,' he said. 'Don't panic. It could be a multitude of things. Just calm down. This is the first of many tests he's going to have before we can form an opinion.' And, yes, one of the possible diagnoses was MS.

They admitted him to Cedars-Sinai, and for his eye he was put on an intravenous drip of steroids over three days.

Ozzy was in England, writing with Tony, and I deliberated about whether I should tell him because it still wasn't definite and I knew it would upset him terribly. But Jack is his son too, and in the end I felt he had to know what the scan had shown. He was devastated. Both me and Ozzy have had a life, but our son's was just beginning.

Jack stayed in that night, then the next day he was given a lumbar puncture. Then it was a case of, Go home and come back in four days for the results.

That was a very emotional week. Ozzy was still away, so I was home alone, trying to stay strong one minute then bursting into tears the next. As for sleeping, forget it. I managed to remain calm when I spoke to Jack on the phone, because I didn't want to burden him further. He was very on edge, not just about the stress of waiting for the results, but because he had a new baby and a wife who'd just given birth. And all the time he was thinking, Oh God, am I even going to be able to walk for much longer?

Everyone's symptoms are different. Some people can't talk, and there was Jack, practically blind in one eye and with a tingling, burning sensation in his legs. He said he felt like boiling water had been poured over them.

After a couple of days, I spoke with the specialist on the phone who said that, having looked at the scans, he was almost sure it was going to be MS. It was just a case of waiting for the tests on the spinal fluid to confirm it.

Lisa was going with him to get the results. But Jack wanted me there as well. We tend to forget that he is still so young – only twenty-six. But I decided I couldn't. I knew I wouldn't be able to hold it together.

And how would it help Jack if I broke down? So I called Ozzy at Tony's studio in Solihull. There are times when a boy needs his father, and this was one of them.

'You have to come back, Ozzy,' I said. 'There's no way I can do this.'

So he did, and Ozzy, Jack and Lisa went into the appointment to be told it was one hundred per cent certain that he had MS. Four months later, we did go for a second opinion, just to be sure. But Jack knew; we all knew.

After the diagnosis, Jack and Lisa went straight home and Ozzy came back to Hidden Hills, where we both cried long into the night. Ozzy had kept so strong during the appointment, but back at home he kept saying, 'If I could take the MS for him, I would.' You don't want a twenty-six-year-old to have that and, at the time, Jack's eye was still very bad. When he spoke to you, you could see his eye trying to focus. He unconsciously developed an eye-half-closed technique; either that, or he would cup his eye completely.

If anything happens to you, you cope with it. But when it's one of your children, you just can't get your head around it. Both Ozzy and I felt so helpless. Our son's adult life was only just beginning and his baby daughter wasn't yet a month old. I was very fortunate in that I had a good friend, Nancy Davis, who knew a great deal about MS. She has had the disease herself for over twenty years, and coming from a very wealthy family she has one of the biggest foundations in America, putting fortunes into raising money and awareness for MS research. So the first person I reached out to was her.

She said to me, 'I was in bed for five months – I couldn't walk, couldn't feel anything past my waist for that entire time. Nothing. Then I woke up one day, *could* feel my legs, so got out of bed and started to walk.'

In other words, it has no pattern; there is no rhythm.

And now, via her foundation, Nancy has been instrumental in getting seven of the nine drugs licensed that are in use today. She's an incredible woman; an inspiration to me and to so many others.

So there *is* hope, but meanwhile Jack lives with the time bomb of thinking it's the MS flaring up every time he gets a headache or a tingling feeling in one of his legs.

When he was first diagnosed, he was very, very angry. It was, 'Why me?' the most natural thing in the world to feel. Then, after a couple of days, the tears came.

How you get MS is still a mystery. Inevitably, Jack began to question himself: all those expeditions to far-flung corners of the world. Had he picked something up? Was it this, was it that? They don't know if it runs in families, and they say probably not, but that didn't stop me from thinking, Oh my God, it's something he's got from me.

That's why research is so important, because so little is known about the disease. Millions of people world-wide suffer from it, women more than men. They used to say that it was an old people's thing. But it isn't. It's simply because it was so hard to spot that people would go for years without being diagnosed.

We recently held a big fundraiser in New York with Nancy – the one where Elton played for us for over an hour. Jack kept saying to Kelly and me, 'Please don't cry,' because it sets him off too, but it's hard not to weaken and sob. There was a seminar the next day, with leading doctors from around the world. They'll tell you the headway they're making, the headway they're not making — and so it's really informative. And there were MS sufferers there who were blind, in wheelchairs, people who couldn't talk properly. And while I admired their courage enormously, all I kept thinking about was my darling son, and maybe having to deal with that one day.

Jack's eye is a lot better now. He has about seventy-five per cent vision and can see certain colours. But that's probably as good as it's going to get, because multiple sclerosis leaves its scars in your body — that's what the name means. Your body will never go back to being a hundred per cent, because you're scarred. The main problem he gets at the moment is numbness and tingling in his legs, though I will never know how much because he rarely complains. He says it's not painful, it's just weird. He describes it as feeling like having warm water trickle down your legs.

He's on medication and injects himself every day. That *is* painful, because the formula is thick, so it takes a long time to inject and leaves inflamed welts on his body. One day he does it in the left leg, then the right leg the next day, then the stomach, and so on. He has to rotate.

The one thing that's certain, following an MS diagnosis, is that you have to do a life change, which includes diet. You have to avoid colds or flu. You shouldn't drink alcohol, though this wasn't an issue for Jack. Now when Jack goes on a plane, he has to sanitise the remote control. You have to be very aware. A virus that a healthy person could shrug off, for him could develop into pneumonia.

Astonishingly, he has remained relentlessly positive, keeping fit and eating well, giving his body the best chance it can have of thwarting the onset of the damn disease. If worse symptoms develop, I'm sure he will find ways to cope with them, because he's such a fighter.

For me, I rationalise his MS in my head by thinking, There's a reason for everything. And maybe if you have it, you've been given it because you're strong enough and you can help others. And maybe, in some tiny little way, you can help other people, and maybe help find out how this wretched thing comes and how you get rid of it.

In the months leading up to Jack's diagnosis, I was back on NBC for *America's Got Talent*. It was in its seventh season.

I absolutely loved it. Not only is it a massive hit show in the States, it's also got a great premise − it's good, clean family entertainment and fun to work on. So I was having a ball doing it. Everything was good.

One day early in 2012, a couple of months before Pearl was born, Jack had had a call from his agent: NBC had been in touch. They were offering him a new show, called *Stars Earn Stripes*, where Special Forces people were pitted against celebrities to see if the celebrity could keep up. They had immediately thought of Jack.

So Jack goes in for a meeting and they fall in love with him, as most people do when they meet my wonderfully straightforward son. He's a regular, nice young man, so it's not hard to like him. Jack was really excited by this project. It could have been tailor-made for him, and he went through all the extreme sports he'd done, all of which had required extensive training and super-fitness, not to mention nerve. The meeting ended with them saying, 'Yes, we definitely want you.'

They explained that the show would be slotted into the programming of the London Olympics later in the summer. He was the first person they cast, and he was over the moon because it was so obviously perfect for him.

The contract arrived and, as is usual with these things, it went back and forth between Jack's lawyers and NBC's while clauses were tweaked. It was in the middle of these negotiations that Jack was diagnosed with MS. By then he had already had the medical for the show, which he'd passed without a hitch. But that was only for standard things like heart, lungs and blood pressure. It was never intended to pick up on something like MS. But once he had the diagnosis, Jack decided to come clean about it. We hadn't spoken publicly at that point, but Jack's agent did the right thing and informed the producers of the show.

A couple of days later, Meredith Ahr, executive vice president at NBC, called me at home. I'd known her for six years, ever since I started on *America's Got Talent*. When I saw her name come up, I felt my heart flip. It was like, 'OK, here we go. Here's the call to fire him.' But no.

'We're so sorry to hear your news, but don't worry. Jack's still very much a part of this. He's family. We will support him the whole way, and if there are any

activities that might be too risky, we'll modify them.'
This was just a personal call, but later she followed up
with an email.

I was close to tears with relief because I knew how
much the show meant to Jack. He had been training so
hard for it. He's a great marksman, and when he realised
he might be impaired by the loss of vision in one eye –
which he has since largely got back – he paid to have
lessons so he could learn to compensate. It seems there
are lots of guys with one eye who are great shots.

He was also working out every single day, to be
ready. For him, this show was the light at the end of his
tunnel; something to focus on other than the disease.
And he could prove to the world that he wasn't going
to let MS beat him.

But as the weeks went on, doubt started to creep into
the voices of those I was dealing with when it came
to finalising the details. The first hint that all was not
well was when Meredith called me. 'We're having a
bit of trouble with insuring him,' she said. I'd already
considered that possibility, and told her that he'd be
covered by his own insurance. That we'd gone into it
and they'd be covered. 'So there's no problem,' I said.

Sensing the way it was going, I even suggested that, if they were still concerned, they might think about using him as a presenter instead. After all, he was already highly experienced. And on the back of *Adrenaline Junkie*, he was perfectly placed to comment on the kind of activities involved. But they said they had given the job to Samantha Harris, who had been co-hosting *Dancing with the Stars*. She happens to be a very nice person. I had nothing against her and she was a perfectly good presenter, but why would you give the job of presenting a show about military activities with Special Forces men to someone who had previously presented a ballroom-dancing show? OK, I know – I am complaining again.

Some days later I had an email from Meredith. She said that she was still trying to find a way for Jack to stay on the show, and was keen to talk to his doctors about 'what parameters, if any, they have to make sure we don't hurt him'. She signed off, 'love and hugs' – still friendly, still apparently doing everything she could to make sure Jack could stay on the show.

By now, Jack had been fitted for his uniform and was due to start sessions on safety and weapons training on 3 and 4 June. Actual taping of the shows would be between 10 and 28 June.

Then, on 2 June, the day before Jack's first training session, I got an email from Chuck Labella, head of talent booking for NBC. He was writing to tell me that 'regretfully' they were unable to move forward with Jack as a part of *Stars Earn Stripes*, because there was 'too much of a health risk'. He went on to tell me how much they all 'love Jack', and hoped to be able to work with him in the future – perhaps on a future season of the show. He closed, 'We are as disappointed as Jack about this news.'

I stared blankly at the screen, unable, or more likely unwilling, to believe what was there. My stomach plummeted. Why were they sending this to me, his mother, while the network had been dealing with his agent and Jack personally? Had they emailed Jack? Why did they leave it until the day before he was due to turn up for work? And fourth, why didn't they keep their word?

Personally I couldn't have cared less about a stupid TV show. But Jack had set so much store by this. It meant too much. It was a chance for him to show the world that a diagnosis of MS didn't mean that his life was over. As for what the doctor had said, they would say of any contestant that dangling someone out of a helicopter into a raging river was dangerous. Working with machine guns was dangerous. Obviously. The reality was that he was as fit now as he'd ever been, apart from the vision in one eye, which was gradually improving.

The first thing I had to do was call Jack. He hadn't received the email. Nor had his agent. Needless to say, Jack was completely devastated.

By now I was seething with the visceral anger of a mother when she feels that one of her children needs protecting. It wasn't the booker's fault. I knew he was just the hapless messenger for the other bastards, those spineless types that occupied the carpeted corridors with fancy nameplates on the doors.

First thing the next morning I called Meredith Ahr, asking what the fuck was going on. She'd given me her word that his diagnosis wouldn't affect anything. As for leaving it till the last minute, that was disgusting. I told her I felt betrayed and disrespected.

Then she said to me, 'Is it about the money? We'll pay him. We'll send him his cheque.'

'Money? He doesn't want your money, he wants a

Back with my good friend Louis Walsh for *The X Factor* judges' houses auditions in 2010.

With Piers Morgan and David Hasselhoff on the judging panel of *America's Got Talent* in 2008.

I loved my time on *AGT* (here in 2011 with a new judge, Howie Mandel) and was very sad when it had to come to an end.

The Apprentice was an incredibly stressful experience. Here I am running around New York, trying to complete one of the ridiculous tasks.

With Lady Gaga and my friend and fellow *Apprentice* contestant Cyndi Lauper at a Mac event in 2010. I was so disappointed in Gaga for not taking a stand when her fans bullied Kelly.

What's a Bieber? Justin Bieber was sweet and professional when we filmed a Superbowl advert with him in 2011.

I have so much fun working on *The Talk*, both on set and backstage. Below L–R: Sheryl Underwood, Sara Gilbert, guest Lucy Liu, me, Aisha Tyler and Julie Chen.

It's a tough job, but someone's gotta do it. Re-enacting the most famous scene from *Ghost*, with the cast of the Broadway show on *The Talk*.

Like father, like son? Above: Ozzy with two-week-old Jack in 1985. Below: Jack with baby Pearl, 2012.

It was strange to be back in Hawaii for Jack and Lisa's wedding, thirty years after Ozzy and I exchanged our own vows in Maui. Of course it was a happy occasion, but I couldn't help reflect on the perilous state of my own marriage.

Celebrating Jack and Lisa's marriage, with their daughter Pearl and (below) bridesmaid and proud sister, Kelly.

It was wonderful to be surrounded by our oldest and closest friends at Jack and Lisa's wedding. Above, Ozzy with (L–R) our manager Colin Newman, Colin's wife Mette, Sabbath bass player Terry 'Geezer' Butler and his wife, and my best friend, Gloria. Below, me with Gloria, Geezer and Colin.

job. He's got something to prove here – that you can still have MS and have a normal life – and the show gave him something to work towards.'

Clearly she had no understanding of the situation Jack was in. As for the money, that was a complete and utter insult.

Something just snapped. 'You're a bunch of fucking arseholes, spineless sons of bitches. And I don't want to be associated with people like you. As for Jack being a liability, how dare you? Jack is not a liability to anyone. But you know what? As much as I love *America's Got Talent*, if it means I have to associate with people like you, I'm leaving.'

'Sharon, I understand why you're upset – you're a mother. But I'm sure you'll feel differently about it once things have calmed down.'

How little they know me, I thought, and put the phone down.

Bear in mind that this is the same network that was more than happy for Bret Michaels to fly in from Phoenix to New York for the *Celebrity Apprentice* finale, despite having just had a brain haemorrhage and – again before the final – being diagnosed with a hole in the heart. On top of that, they had always known that he was severely diabetic. Double standards, or what?

I waited a couple of hours and then I called Paul Telegdy, Meredith's boss at NBC and President of NBC Entertainment, and it went from bad to ugly fast.

'You know what?' I told him. 'You're a bunch of unimaginative arseholes. You could turn this show into something else, something worthwhile that proves that people who have disabilities can still win. You could make it a different type of programme. And another thing,' I continued, '*anybody* who will listen to my story, I am telling. I am going to sing like a fucking canary to the world – whoever will listen. If you think I'm going to be quiet, you are fucking nuts.'

'We won't be threatened, Sharon.'

'Telling the truth is not making a threat. Ozzy and I are going to hold a press conference and tell everyone what you've done to our son.' My comment was total bullshit. I just said it for the drama. I was in full drama queen mode. In fact I remember mumbling something about how Ozzy was on his way to New York to appear live on *Letterman*. Again that was all bullshit.

The call ended with him saying something like, 'Do

what you want to do,' and the phone clicked off. He followed up this conversation with an email, in which he said he was 'strongly suggesting' that I limit my communication with them, and instead deal with them via my and Jack's agents. Apparently it was 'extremely vexing' for them to hear 'ill-informed, erroneous' accusations, when they were 'trying to help'. He went on to say that what I was saying bordered on defamation, and was a 'complete waste' of their time.

How can the truth be perceived as 'defamation'?

My *America's Got Talent* contract meant that I was locked in to do the live shows in New York because I had already spent two months filming the audition stages. If I had pulled at that point, they would undoubtedly have sued me. But staying on didn't mean I was going to be submissive. It didn't mean I had to play that bullshit lovey-dovey TV game. It didn't mean I had to blow smoke up anyone's arse.

The following week I had to fly to New York with these people to start filming the live shows. As usual it was a private plane, an eight-seater, with just the executives and me and my assistant on board. As the car pulled up on the tarmac at Van Nuys airport, in the valley, there they were, with shit-eating grins on their faces: Meredith Ahr and Bob Greenblatt, the new head of NBC, who I had never met in my life.

So Meredith goes, 'Sharon! Sharon, how *lovely* to see you!' As for Greenblatt, I gave him my best Bette Davis face and ignored his extended hand, which was preparing to shake mine. I looked at them both, turned my head then got into the plane. I never said a word.

Meredith turned to my assistant, Julie, who was following behind and said, 'So this is how it's going to be, is it?' Yes, missus, you got it. We sat on that plane for five hours. You could have cut the atmosphere with a butter knife. Not a word was spoken.

It was the journey from hell.

The following day was the first *America's Got Talent* show live from New York. I was in the elevator going down to the stage from my dressing room, and when the doors opened there stood none other than Paul Telegdy, who'd instructed me to communicate solely through my agent. He had his arms outstretched as if he was about to clasp me to his bosom: 'Shazza!' he said, acting as if nothing had ever happened. And I was like, 'Fuck off,' and I shooed him away with my hands as if he was a fly landing on a turd. I never looked at him or spoke to him throughout the entire series, and we were there for ten weeks.

I totally understood the awkward situation they were in as a network. But they were wrong in constantly reassuring us that everything would be fine. They were wrong in leaving it till the day before to pull the rug from under Jack's feet. And then they were very, very wrong when we went public, when they denied he was ever going to be a participant, which they did. *It was never a deal. There was never a contract, so what was all the fuss about?* They may have had a problem but, as executives representing a public corporation, a network that had had a six-year relationship with me, they handled it horribly.

I don't hold NBC responsible as a corporation. It's the executives who made the decision I have no respect for.

In fact, the stance they took made them look ridiculous. Why would Jack and I make up the story that he'd been cast if he hadn't? There was a contract – unsigned, admittedly – but why would we make up that story? What would have been the advantage to us? It made no sense.

All of it could have been avoided, all the ugliness and the public battles, if NBC had been gracious enough to be truthful and say, 'We're not happy with these circumstances; unfortunately we're going to have to let Jack go, and here's a small donation to MS research.' We would have been upset, but we would have understood.

America's Got Talent didn't finish until the middle of September. When there was one week of the series left, I asked my agent to contact NBC to see if they could give me a proper send-off. If you've been on a show for the time I had, they'll give you a goodbye. They'll put together a reel of your best moments and wish you well.

They refused. Fine. On the final day, I'd gone through different scenarios in my head as to what I should do, as we were going live. Should I go gracefully? Or should I make a scene? And if so, how? Was it going to be dramatic – a great Hollywood ending? Or just dignified. Even sitting there as the minutes ticked down, I didn't know how to handle it. It ended up that one of the finalists who didn't win was a little girls' dancing group, and one of the little girls said to Nick Cannon as they were leaving the stage, 'We don't want to leave,' and she was crying. That was my cue. I interrupted the interview which, remember, was going out live, and said, 'I don't want to leave either, but I have to, just like you. This is my last show. So hold my hand and we'll go together.' When the winner was announced, a dog act I'd been campaigning for since they first appeared, I got up from my seat, took my shoes off and ran up on stage, which I was not meant to do. I then proceeded to prance about, doing the most ridiculous skipping movements. Basically, it was my *fuck you* to NBC. I saw the little girl, and we hugged. She had no idea of the role she'd played in my departure.

Anyway, there's a great saying, 'Stand by the bank of the river long enough and you will see the bodies of your enemies float by.'

When the *Stars Earn Stripes* show began to air, Desmond Tutu and various other Nobel Peace Prize winners tried to get it banned on the grounds that it glorified war, and they encouraged people to campaign to get it off the air. They didn't succeed, but it tanked in the ratings anyway, as it was considered to be in bad taste. Karma is a bitch.

11

Body and Soul

Maybe it's time to start growing old gracefully?

I was rapidly approaching my sixtieth birthday, but it's fair to say that not every part of my body was of quite the same vintage. Over the years, there's not much I haven't had tweaked, stretched, peeled, lasered, veneered, enhanced or removed altogether. But as I write this, I can tell you that, hand on original, sixty-year-old heart, I won't be having any more cosmetic procedures. The neck lift during my mastectomy was my last, and my days of growing old disgracefully are well and truly over. There are two main reasons for this.

First, my family, and Ozzy especially, are terrified about me going under a general anaesthetic unless I absolutely have to. That old heart I mentioned? It's endured enough surgical procedures already, not to mention the strain of several courses of chemotherapy. There's only so much the human body can take, and I feel that mine has already been pushed to its limits. It doesn't need any more stress placed on it in my endless pursuit of youth.

But second, my cancer, the mastectomy and, more importantly, Jack's illness, put everything into perspective for me. When you witness your own or your child's body having to fight a genuine threat, choosing to put it through the mill for the purposes of vanity seems beyond idiotic. Looking back now, I am genuinely disturbed by how many times I have been under the surgeon's knife in pursuit of a physical 'perfection' that doesn't exist.

People often talk about having 'good days' and 'bad days' when they look in the mirror, 'Oh, I'm having a "fat" day,' or, 'Wow, I look really great this morning.' Well, I had *never* looked in the mirror and liked what I saw. Never. In my mind, I had always been fat, hairy, with little legs and disproportionately large tits, and nothing I could ever do to my body would change that. But boy, did I try.

Body and Soul

My obsession with having cosmetic surgery is well documented, particularly since I started doing television and became better known. I have always felt that if you're in the public eye, you should be honest about what you've had done so that other women don't have unrealistic expectations. They should know that there's nothing natural about it, that it costs shitloads of money to look that way and that you are putting your body through brutal surgical procedures.

I was having things done long *before* I became famous. I started altering myself even before I was married. I had what I called *National Geographic* tits – very pendulous – so I first had them reduced and lifted in 1978. I was a bit of a pioneer. Then there was my first facelift in 1987, when I was just thirty-five years old! Trouble is, because of my yo-yoing weight (I would get big then I would lose the weight really quickly), I would be left with excess saggy skin. So it was this eternal merry-go-round of hate myself, eat; hate myself, diet; hate myself, have surgery; hate myself, eat . . . you get the picture. I was every cosmetic surgeon's perfect customer. I should have been given a fucking loyalty card.

Then there was another facelift, around 2002, I think, and over the years I have had my legs lifted, my arms lifted, my breasts done again and my tummy tucked after I had the gastric band. Much of the surgery was because my fluctuating weight left me with hideously droopy skin. And I thought if I just had perfect breasts, then my *life* would be perfect, too. Dumb, huh?

The trouble is, you start doing it, then you come round from the operation and think, OK, that was pretty easy. Then you look in the mirror and, although you're not completely perfect, you quite like what you see and that gives you a bit of confidence. Then that confidence eventually starts to ebb and you miss it, and the next thing you know, you're back having another op to boost yourself up again. It's a vicious and gory cycle.

I used to have Botox and fillers, too, but not any more. It's terrible stuff. I had fillers just before Lisa's baby shower and a couple of days later, when I looked at the photographs of me, I was shocked. From certain angles, I looked *really* odd. Very plastic. My eyes were like slits, my cheeks puffy. I looked like a completely different person, as if I was wearing a mask. There I was, supposedly celebrating the imminent arrival of my granddaughter, and my face was virtually incapable of expression.

I don't think I'm as bad as some women, like Jocelyn 'Bride of' Wildenstein. But I had definitely fallen into the trap of thinking I looked OK without frown or laughter lines, not realising that the minute you start talking or trying to smile, you look like an alien that's lost contact with the mother ship.

For me, the baby-shower pictures were a defining moment. I thought, Holy crap, it was only a few injections and look at the *state* of me. It was at that point that I decided no more Botox and fillers, thank you very much. I'm *so* over it. It felt like liquid concrete that had completely changed the angle of my features, and not in a good way. Unless, of course, you want to look like a fucking hamster.

I'm pleased to report that my face has settled down since then and I can actually *move* the bloody thing.

There's nothing worse than someone having everything they want done, then turning around to everyone else and preaching that they shouldn't do the same, I realise that. But after advocating cosmetic surgery and non-surgical procedures for so long, I feel it is only right to pass on that my opinion has changed. It's a fine line, really. If you hate your nose or ears and they make you feel self-conscious, then having them tweaked or pinned back will probably change your life. I get that, and if either of my daughters felt that way, I would say, 'Go right ahead.' Similarly, I know what it's like to hate your tits, so if you're a young woman and you genuinely feel embarrassed taking your top off in front of someone, then who am I to say that you shouldn't do something about it with a one-off procedure?

What I'm talking about is women like me who hate what they see in the mirror and will keep on having surgery because we don't know how to stop.

Wrinkles and sagging are part of life, I realise that now; they're part of *you*. And every time you go under the knife for vanity, you are slicing off yet more of your self-worth, too. Far better to find other ways of trying to feel comfortable with who you are. Jack's diagnosis and my mastectomy were both lines in the sand for me, but turning sixty may be part of it, as well as becoming a grandmother and finally realising that there is so much more to life than fretting about your droopy bits.

In between my many cosmetic surgery operations, I would also embark on some of the most ludicrous diets known to woman. There was the gastric band, of course, but I have also done powders, pills, the cactus diet, the cabbage soup diet, the purée diet, the fasting-every-other-day diet, the South Beach diet. You name it, I have been on it.

The lightest I have ever been is 107 pounds (seven stone, nine pounds), but even then I would never be the girl to wear the shortest skirt, or even a bikini on the beach. I have never strutted around naked in front of my husband – I'm always swathed in something because I don't like my body. The perfect era for me would have been Victorian times when they took ladies to the water's edge in a carriage and you dropped into the sea unseen.

Now I'm on the Atkins diet and it seems to be working for me. My weight has started to drop steadily rather than rapidly, which is an encouraging sign. My experience has always been that losing the pounds isn't that hard, it's *maintaining* the weight loss that's the tricky bit. And you have more chance of success if you have lost the weight slowly and sensibly. This is the first diet

I have done where I can actually go to a restaurant and order something from the menu, like steak and vegetables, or fish.

Ozzy tried it too, and he lost a lot of weight initially, though he goes back and forth on it – much like I do. Ozzy cares very much about his weight, with good reason. Performing at the level he does, doing two-hour shows a night, he needs to be a comfortable weight. And to achieve that, Ozzy works out every single day, obsessively.

I, however, will have a little voice in my head that says, *Go to the gym, go to the gym*, and I will think, In a minute, in a minute. I need someone to be standing next to me, constantly prodding me in the back until I do it. For the last year I have worked with a personal trainer. Her name is Michelle Woolf, known to her clients as Woolfie, and we've become great mates. Even when I moan and say I can't do it, she will come and grab me and push me into the gym and if I moan too much, she'll make me do double.

Over the first three months I steadily lost twenty-five pounds – almost two stone – and had just eight more pounds to lose to reach my ideal weight. Then it was down to four. Nearly there! It was all looking so promising and then I sabotaged myself by starting to eat junk food again. Some people starve themselves when they're unhappy or feeling a bit low, but I comfort-eat. I know when I'm doing it that I really shouldn't, that I will put on weight that I have worked so hard to lose, but I still do it because it feels *soooo* good at the time. And then I disappoint myself.

I went for therapy a few times to try and get to the bottom of it but frankly, I got bored of talking about myself. I just wanted to scream, 'Can we talk about something else now?' Or I'd find myself saying things I didn't really feel, just for the sake of it, to fill the silence in the room. So I stopped going.

By the time you get to my age, you can pretty much analyse yourself anyway. The plain facts are that it's not just about dieting. It's about a lifestyle change, which means mind, body and soul. Yes, you can lose weight – anyone can lose weight – but you cannot maintain it without life changes, which means exercise. You must take care of your body. It's only taken me sixty years to accept this and to stop the voices inside my head saying, 'Eat that cake! You can start the diet on Monday.'

However much I crave carbs and sabotage my diet occasionally, I always have a cut-off point in my head now. After all my medical problems, I know that I can't go back to being 230 pounds (sixteen and a half stone) again, it's too unhealthy. I just can't allow myself to become that person again. In many ways, I'm fighting pretty lousy odds, anyway. My mother and father were both prone to weight problems and had short, stumpy legs. Some people inherit a lump sum from their parents; I just got a lumpy body.

So I'm short and I'm small-boned, and when I'm in one of my 'big' phases, it's all fat that you can see. Never mind the aesthetics; that's so unhealthy for someone of my age. When you're too heavy, your knees go, your back goes, your feet swell. And I don't want to find myself struggling to stand up, so that's why I *always* go back on the diet after a self-inflicted sabotage. Besides, I hate waking up one morning to find that the blouse I really like suddenly won't do up any more, or my trousers are too tight, or my favourite ring won't slip on to my big, fat, puffy finger.

When I'm being a good girl, I have egg and bacon for breakfast, then when I'm at *The Talk* I invariably have a salad of avocado, beansprouts, tomatoes, maybe some carrots. It really does fill me up, and it works. *If* I stick to it.

If I'm being a bad girl, I will stuff my face with pasta, chips or – my absolute downfall every time – strawberry cream cake. God, I love it. If it's there in the fridge, I just can't *not* eat it and, if I'm feeling a bit down on myself, I will ask my housekeeper Saba to buy one so that it's there when I get home.

There is one habit I have managed to kick. Every single morning, without fail, I would drink a huge glass of Coca-Cola to get me going. The full-on sugared stuff, not the diet version. Whenever I felt tired I would drink it, get the sugar rush, then get the slump. So then I would drink it again to bring me out of the slump. But since I have been doing Atkins, I haven't touched it. In fact, I don't have fizzy drinks at all, which is a massive bonus to my diet because, sugar-wise, they are dreadful. I have also trained myself to eat fruit, which I *never* used to do, and I'm getting better at eating vegetables, although I accept that I will never be the kind of person who chews on a stick of celery because I actually enjoy it.

Unbreakable

I'm not a beauty or fashion icon, I'm just a normal person who got lucky. I can scrub up pretty well for my age, with the help of a good make-up artist and some flattering lighting, but the rest of the time I honestly couldn't give a toss what I look like. I often go out without make-up on looking a right old sight.

When Jack and Lisa were moving into their new house, I was helping to shift boxes and clean floors, like all mothers do for their kids. After a while, we were all starving, so we went to Madeo's Restaurant in West Hollywood, and when we came out the paparazzi were outside. I was wearing a pair of baggy old jeans and a T-shirt, and had a scarf on my head because my hair was all over the place. The next thing I know, I've got Louis Walsh on the phone taking the piss and calling me a scruffy old cow. How dare he!

12

Here We Go Again

Ozzy and I renewing our vows in 2002, twenty years after
our first wedding. I would never have imagined then that our
thirtieth wedding anniversary would be the beginning of one
of the worst periods in our turbulent marriage.

On 4 July 2012, my husband and I celebrated our thirtieth wedding anniversary.

I would like to be able to tell you that he organised the delivery of a vast bouquet of flowers before taking me for a candlelit supper for two.

But I'm married to Ozzy Osbourne, whose capacity for fucking up is legendary. So, suffice to say that it was one of the most anticlimactic, frustrating, distressing days of my life. And given what I have already been through, that's saying something.

I was working in New York on *America's Got Talent*, and Ozzy had just finished the summer festival dates, which were meant to be Black Sabbath, but due to Tony's illness became Ozzy and Friends. The 4th of July is of course a national holiday in America for Independence Day, a fitting occasion for celebration.

The plan was that Ozzy would fly out from London the night before and we'd spend the day just hanging out together in my suite at the Greenwich Hotel in Tribeca. I was looking forward to doing nothing, but was apprehensive about the imminent arrival of my husband, who had been particularly stroppy with me of late. Nothing I ever did seemed to be right and, on the rare occasions he was home, I kept out of his way. It was safer for both of us.

The day before he was due to arrive, I got a call from Pete Mertens, a dear friend of both of ours. He'd gone to school with Ozzy and Tony Iommi and, in one of those small-world coincidences, I had met him independently when I worked for ELO and he was one of their roadies. So we all go back a long way.

Now retired and living in Laguna, California, he's one of the biggest jokers there is, so when I hear his voice it always makes me smile.

'Pete! How you doing?'

We got the usual social niceties out of the way and then he cleared his throat, sounding slightly awkward.

'Sharon, Ozzy keeps texting me to ask if I can get him any drugs. Is everything OK?'

I half laughed, waiting for the confirmation that this was Pete's idea of a wind-up. But none came. No laughing matter, it turned out to be the tip-off that set in motion the next gut-churning episode in my box-of-chocolates marriage. You never know what you're going to get next.

I had told Ozzy weeks before that when he landed in New York on the night of 3 July, I would most likely still be on the set of *America's Got Talent*, but that I'd only be about an hour behind him.

'Just get unpacked, have a bath, get into bed and I'll be there,' I'd said.

So come the night, I was on set and we had just gone to a commercial break when my assistant Julie brings me my phone. It's Ozzy, calling from the hotel.

'You arsehole. I've flown halfway round the fucking world and you're not fucking here.'

I had a microphone on and either side of me were the other two judges, Howard Stern and Howie Mandel. As I had done so many times in the past, I smiled sweetly and pretended that everything was just hunky-dory in my world.

'Oh, hi darling! I can't waaaaaait to see yoooooooo-oooooou. Lovely . . . lovely. OK, I'll be there in an hour. Mwah.'

Click. Oh fuck, I thought, it's going to be a rough night.

The first thing that happens to me when I'm emotional is that my stomach starts to knot.

Luckily, *America's Got Talent* was not due back on air for another two minutes, so I rushed off to the loo, praying that I would get to the end of that night's show without betraying how upset I was. By some miracle, I managed it.

By the time I arrived back at the hotel, Ozzy was in bed, watching TV. He started on me straight away.

'Well, if this is the way it's going to be, then our fucking anniversary is just a fucking joke. You've got to fucking rethink our life,' he ranted.

Everything was my fault. Me, me, me, me, always fucking *me*. I already had a plan of action in my head, and knew what I wanted to do. So I didn't retaliate, I simply took it all, removed my make-up and got in beside him, waiting for him to pop a sleeping pill that would release me from this verbal onslaught. As soon as he was out cold, I picked up his phone and started scrolling through the texts, looking for evidence of what Pete had told me.

Normally, I would never do something like that. Ozzy has kept journals from the day we met; he has bookcases full of them. But I would no more rifle through them than fly to the moon. It's something I have always taught my kids: *never* snoop at someone's computer, mobile phone or diaries because you will only find something that might hurt you. And besides, it's an invasion of their privacy.

Ozzy knew I felt that way, which is probably why he didn't see the need to delete anything. But right then, in New York and about to celebrate our thirtieth wedding anniversary, I was a desperate woman.

It didn't take long and boy, did I find a load of ugly shit. There were texts going back months, asking people to get him drugs and saying, 'Don't tell the old girl.' It was all there in black and white, everything I knew I would find but had desperately hoped I wouldn't. Without evidence, I could bury my head in the sand and pretend it wasn't happening, just as I had done about so many uncomfortable truths in my life. But there it was, incontrovertible. After doing so well with sobriety, and despite everything he had promised both to me and the kids, my husband was abusing again.

Looking back, I think I was in shock, because I *still* didn't say anything to him. All I kept thinking was, Let's get through our anniversary day tomorrow and I'll worry about this afterwards. Also, I was wary about confronting him in a public place because I had no idea how he would react.

The next morning, I woke first and lay stock still for a few minutes, staring at the ceiling and trying to get my head straight. If we manage to have a nice day together, I thought, then perhaps this can all be sorted out. But no.

Our precious day together – the celebration of three decades, three gorgeous children and everything else we had achieved – was just a blank.

He lay on the sofa for most of the day, watching TV. He hated the 'fucking hotel', hated the 'fucking food', hated being in New York. He was tired, he'd just finished his tour, he wanted to go to LA, why had I made him come to New York . . . The list of complaints was endless, the vitriol unrelenting. And that's what I endured *all* day for our thirtieth anniversary.

Meanwhile, our family and friends were calling to congratulate us on making it to three decades. With a Herculean effort, I managed to sound like we were having a great time, just holed up in our hotel room like two lovebirds with no desire to see the outside world, though given Ozzy's moods of late, the kids would have known that, at best, we were perhaps managing to get through the day without bickering.

I had had a belt buckle made for him, mounted with a gold cross and inscribed on the back, *Happy 30th anniversary. Here's to the next 30.* But I didn't give it to him. I still haven't, to this day. I never will. It now lives in the safe. If we make it to forty, maybe. Not only had he not bought me anything, he never even acknowledged what day it was. He acted as if, to him, it was just another shit day in another shit hotel. Except that I knew there was nothing wrong with the hotel, or with me. It was his craving for drugs talking, just as, I now realised, it had been causing his recent mood swings. As it happened, Michele Anthony and her mum Harriet had sent Ozzy and me a chocolate cake for our anniversary. So I ate it. All of it, and loved every bite. I didn't let him near it. As for my husband, he just wanted any excuse to get the fuck out.

The next day we had a scheduled appointment to see an MS specialist in Boston. Jack met us there that morning. We stayed for three days. The specialist confirmed Jack's diagnosis – which we all knew anyway, but there is always that seed of hope. But for me, all I felt was relief – relief to be with Jack. Ozzy came with us, but he was closed off emotionally. He was there in body, but not in mind. After we got the diagnosis we flew right back to LA, all three of us. Ozzy and I returned to Hidden Hills, and Jack to Lisa and Pearl.

If I had expected him to be contrite after his behaviour in New York, I was sorely mistaken. He was as foul to me as ever, making no attempt to hide his irritation at my mere presence, calling me a fucking this and a fucking that. Again, I soaked it all up, watching and waiting.

By late afternoon, he was absorbed in something on television, so I wandered into the room we referred to as his bunker, where he would spend hours doing his art or poring over books and rock magazines. He kept his journals in there, so I found the ones covering the time from when he was writing in England to being away on tour, and I flicked through them. His scrawl was virtually illegible, but I could make out several references to drinking and drugs.

Then I headed for our bathroom and went through his medicine bag. It was full of pills, prescribed by every fucking doctor in Denmark, Norway, France, Italy, Germany . . . bags and bags and bags of them. All perfectly legal, but none of them necessary.

It was mostly Ritalin, the drug for ADHD, attention-deficit hyperactivity disorder. Surprise surprise, according to experts it possesses some pharmacological similarities to cocaine. There were sleeping pills, Valium and pills that I later discovered were speed. This was on top of the medication I *did* know about for high blood pressure, and the steroids he was taking because he'd been having problems with his voice.

I sat there for several seconds, staring at this pharmaceutical pyramid piled in front of me, trying to get to grips with the enormity of what I was about to deal with. Then I packed it all away again and planned my next move.

That night, once he had taken his sleeping tablet, I knew there was a sedated window of opportunity before he zonked out completely.

'So what have you been drinking?' I asked. And he told me. Everything: beer, vodka, wine – whatever he could get his hands on. Then I progressed to the chemist's shop that was in his bag.

'And why are you taking all these pills?'

'To get fucked up.'

Perhaps the sleeping pill had dulled his will to fight.

I sat there for quite some time, studying the sleeping face of the man I had been through so much with, yet right at this moment felt I barely knew. I didn't feel anger, just an overwhelming sense of weariness. Wasn't life supposed to be easier as we got older? Weren't we all supposed to mellow and look back on our wild days with a sense of fondness, but grateful that they were behind us? Yet here was my husband, sixty-bloody-four and still behaving like a teenage rock star.

Before I knew it, it was 4 a.m. Too exhausted for rational thought, I felt only an overwhelming desire to get the hell out, away from the source of my pain. I packed a suitcase, scooped up the dogs – making sure I took his special dog Rocky, to hurt him – and loaded them into the car. In just a couple of hours I was due at *The Talk* studios for that day's show. What the fuck was I going to do?

Taking a deep breath, I stopped at the side of the road and called Angelica, the CBS Head of Daytime, my boss and a very bright young woman. I told her everything that was going on and said that I just couldn't muster the strength to do the show.

'Listen, Sharon, do what you've got to do, sort out whatever's going on in your life and then come back to work.' She was heavenly to me.

Now the only immediate problem to solve was, where did I go?

We loved the house in Hidden Hills, but just as the kids had warned us, it was too cut off out there. If you're taking life easy, it's perfect. But Ozzy was either writing the album or on tour, and I was doing a daily show in central LA, and the location of the house was adding around ninety minutes to my journey time. Invariably we'd end up staying in our small, one-bedroom apartment in Sierra Towers. It was a fun and interesting place to be – Elton had a place there, as well as Courteney Cox, and Cher – but it was tiny, and when me and Ozzy were there, plus our house-keeper Saba and probably one or two of the kids at any given time, it was ridiculously cramped. So a couple of months earlier I had put Hidden Hills on the market and found a readily available house to rent in Walden Drive, Beverly Hills.

It was a Spanish-style, two-storey house, set back from the road behind a cluster of small trees and bushes. Consequently it was pretty gloomy inside, which proved rather fitting considering the state of our marriage. This meant that, having left my husband sleeping at Hidden Hills, I still had two other properties to choose from, but instead I checked into the Beverly Hills Hotel. I'd been staying there since I was a teenager and it had always been my home from home in LA. I felt comfortable there.

What was I to do? Was I to tell the kids? Was I to tell Tony and Geezer? Was I to tell our friends? I was numb. Ozzy had been clean for seven years. It had taken so long to get there. So much heartache and pain for us. So much effort from him to get himself sober. Every day it's hard work to battle those demons, and he'd done it.

I had just presumed that he was sailing. That he was on the right road. That he was on skis going down the perfect slope. He'd got his dignity back, he'd regained his respect. He was a stronger man, mentally and physically. Now he'd thrown all that away. And at this point in his life, he was a man with great principles. He was a force to be reckoned with. He wasn't playing the victim or a clown any more, he was his own man. And he was a beacon of hope for so many people in positions similar to his; living proof that you never give up.

Through all of these dark thoughts I remembered everything I'd learnt going to family week at rehab. That this is a disease. A devastating, painful disease. I just wanted to take him in my arms and cuddle him and tell him, 'It's going to be all right.' The saddest thing was having to tell the kids and our friends. I knew I had to. To keep it secret would have been the worst thing to do because you're protecting that person. And everybody was so disappointed and sad for him.

Over the next couple of days, Ozzy left Hidden Hills and went to the house in Walden Drive. And so I met up with him. His attitude at that time was, 'What the fuck? I had a slip. Forget it. I'm never doing it again.' But his 'slip', I calculated, had lasted seven months. From his journals I'd found out that he'd started drinking the previous January. Seven months of abusing himself and living a lie and fucking with my head out of guilt. Because every time he saw me he was cold and confrontational, looking for an argument, looking to fight. I'd been thirty-two years with this man. He'd always said we were like bread and butter. We were a team. Again, I wasn't going to walk away because my heart went out to him. And besides, we had a wedding to look forward to. Jack was getting married on 7 October.

So I said to him, get back on your AA twelve-step programme. We'll give you all the emotional support you need. Your family, your friends, Tony and Geezer, we're all here for you.

I let him live with that, to think about the implications, for a couple of days. And then I went to stay with Jack, giving Ozzy time to himself. This time my kids were there to support me. The timing just sucked with everything that had gone on that year. We didn't need this shit, any of us.

I went back to Ozzy, a couple of days after he promised me that he would go right back to day one of the AA twelve-step recovery programme and work on staying clean and sober. Given everything I had learnt about his addiction over the years, I knew that for Ozzy it was the only thing that worked. It's a code you live by, dealing not only with your addiction but also with you as a human being: the way you think, the way you behave and the way you treat other people in your life. You either live by it, or you don't. It's like the Ten Commandments, except that there are twelve of them.

Despite their sadness and their disappointment in him, the kids were very much of the mindset that we all had to help him get through this dark period. None of them urged me to leave him. They were upset with their dad for all the bullshit, for not being honest, but then people who are using don't tend to be.

Now that everything was out in the open, it explained a lot, because as much as he hadn't been there for me in recent months, he hadn't been there for them either. It's the knock-on effect. Dad's not coming for Sunday lunch; Dad's not coming to Aimee/Kelly/Jack's because he's tired; Dad's sleeping; Dad's stressed because of the album; Dad's under so much pressure. They had heard this for so much of their lives, and recently they'd been hearing it again.

I would see their faces, especially the girls'. Dad doesn't call. Dad doesn't text. Have I done something wrong? So even though there was now an explanation for all those disappointments, it was a fine line between a sense of relief that it wasn't something *they'd* done and a sadness that yet again so much quality time they could have shared with him had been lost to his addiction.

And me? I felt a wave of relief too. After all, I could now tell myself that all of the vitriol I had endured for the past few months hadn't been because he didn't love me any more. The slow and painful disintegration of our marriage hadn't happened because of anything *I* had done or hadn't done, it was because of the drugs, the alcohol, *his* addiction.

'Sharon, I'm working this programme. I'm clean, I will stay clean and I will do *whatever* I have to do to keep this family together,' he told me.

'OK, but I need to see *real* change, Ozzy. I need to see progress. I need to see you grow as a human being.

When it's one of the kids' birthdays and I ask you what we should do for them, have a fucking view other than, "I dunno." In other words, rejoin the world or don't bother.'

Anyway, Ozzy stayed at the dark house on Walden Drive and for the next couple of weeks, I dotted between Jack and Lisa's place, the hotel, Aimee's for a while and being back out with *America's Got Talent*, honouring my contract until I could get the hell out of there.

In the meantime, it was Aimee who came up with the idea that her parents should go to therapy together, for what my generation would call marriage guidance. We had never done it before; the old Ozzy wouldn't even have contemplated it. But to my surprise, he agreed to start straight away.

He really tried hard to answer the questions and open up. But I could tell that he absolutely hated it. He'd done therapy in the past, but that was to do with addiction. This was different. He didn't like exposing himself, and I get that. Ozzy has always found it difficult to talk about emotions.

Inevitably, we'd miss an appointment, or forget one.

Then he was out of town, or I was out of town, and so it just got whittled away. In the end, I think we managed about four sessions. And what did I learn about my husband after thirty years of sharing the same bed? Not a fucking thing.

But what the hell; I moved back into Walden Drive anyway, and we muddled along for a bit until Ozzy started work, recording *13* with Tony and Geezer and Rick in Malibu. At least I had something to look forward to. A wedding in Hawaii.

13

Something Old, Something New

The groom and his proud mum.

Jack and Lisa were married on 7 October 2012, at the Four Seasons Resort in Hualalai, Big Island, Hawaii.

Hawaii is the most exquisite of places. In fact, Ozzy and I got married on the island of Maui in 1982, and they say that if you get married in Hawaii you will return there constantly. And it's certainly been true for us. We must have been back at least twenty times since the kids were born, and they have spent so many joyous holidays there, with friends and family members joining us, over the years. It was a huge part of all our lives.

Lisa had never been to Hawaii, but Jack had painted

this picture for her of beauty and romance and she was ecstatic to be getting married there. Jack knew exactly what he wanted. The previous year he'd been to the wedding of a friend who got married on the beach under two arching trees that meet in the middle, known as 'the love trees'. The beach faced west and they had got married at sunset. Although it had been very low-key, Jack said it was magnificent and that, if ever he got married, it would be there.

The great thing about having a wedding away from home is that you don't feel obliged to ask everyone you have ever met, and nobody feels slighted if they're not invited.

So it was a comparatively small wedding. Small but very special: forty-eight of Jack's closest family and friends flew in three days before. This was going to be a real celebration. Unlike ours.

The night before the big day, we all gathered on the beach for a candlelit supper. It was perfection. The sea shimmered in the light of a dozen or more tiki torches, six-foot-high flaming sentinels running the length of the beach. As the staff made the final preparations, we sat barefoot on the sand, silently watching baby turtles that had just hatched going in and out of the surf, trying out their new swimming skills. It was the perfect night, warm yet with a breeze coming off the ocean. The restaurant behind us was open to the sky – later, the stars – and the sounds of the sea. The dinner was Lisa's, from the flower arrangements on the tables and the music to the food that we ate. It was all done with such delicacy and care. She's only twenty-four and this was the first time she'd ever hosted anything like it, and she did it absolutely beautifully.

During the wonderful dinner, I spent my time table-hopping, catching up with friends I hadn't seen in a while and getting to know Lisa's family. As the night wore on, with the sound of laughter and tinkling glasses in my ears, I walked towards the shore, sat cross-legged on the sand and gazed back at the glow of the party that lit up the night. Amid the throng of guests, I made out Lisa and Jack sitting with Lisa's parents. They looked so happy. It was as if I was seeing them in slow motion. They were laughing and relaxed, the sounds of their voices lost in the general hubbub. And looking at them, so happy and carefree, part of me was jealous. But another part of me was thankful, grateful that my son had married into this warm, close-knit family. They were all grounded people.

Inevitably, I thought back to my own wedding, over thirty years before. It was the same sea, the same landscape but it was as different as night from day. Ours was a typical rock 'n' roll wedding. No friends, just band and crew, and of course my miserable parents with their sarcastic remarks throughout the day. And I thought too of my dress, held together with two safety pins, and of my wedding night spent alone while my new husband was on the piss. And I was thankful for having Lisa in Jack's life.

I started to cry, and didn't stop for about thirty-six hours.

Breakfast the next morning had the air of a festival about it. Everyone knew each other. Children were rushing around, and the atmosphere was heady with excitement. Jack and Lisa had wanted the ceremony to feel intimate, and it was. No strangers, only people who were there because they were important in Jack and Lisa's lives. I know it's a cliché, but, Osbournes or Stellys, we really were one big happy family. Around us, the staff were busy threading fairy lights through the love trees. The canopy where Lisa and Jack would make their vows was being laced with exotic flowers. Lisa and her mum and sisters were having their hair done in the beauty salon, having manicures and pedicures. I was catching up with my niece Gina who had come all the way from England with her husband and their gorgeous children, who were now as besotted with Pearl as the rest of us.

And then the head of hotel security said he needed a word with Jack and me. There were now about ten paparazzi, he explained, staking out positions around the grounds. As they were booked into the hotel, nothing could be done to stop them. In any case, the beaches were all public. Under Hawaiian law, they had as much right to be there as we did. I couldn't bear it. Everything had been planned around a wedding on the beach between the love trees. The children had grown up with the story of Ozzy's and my wedding on the beach in Maui, and Jack had so wanted to do it the same way. But the last thing in the world they needed was to have complete strangers clicking away during the most solemn and joyous occasion of their young lives. So, with only a few hours to go, we worked with the hotel to come up with another location, which was private while keeping that special ambience of marrying in the open air.

While the ceremony had been planned to take place on the beach, the reception was to be held in a private area of the hotel grounds. So the decision was made to turn that into the wedding area. Everything had to be moved, the most complicated feature being the canopy with its festoons of tropical ferns and flowers.

I can't deny that I was desperately disappointed, because I so wanted Jack's vision of a wedding on a beach. That being said, it was still a magical ceremony. Lisa's niece and nephews were the flower girl and pages. Her bridesmaids were her three sisters and Kelly. And Jack's best man was Jamie Heffron, who he first met at nursery school aged three, and who he's been friends with ever since.

The wedding took place one hour before sunset, in front of an altar crafted from the island's ferns, hibiscus and orchids. The lawn beneath their feet was scattered with thousands of white orchid petals, fashioning a floral aisle between the rows of simple bamboo chairs placed either side for guests.

Something Old, Something New

Ozzy accompanied Lisa's mother down the aisle, I accompanied Jack down the aisle and Lisa's father naturally walked her down the aisle. They were married by Ryan de Rouen, Lisa's brother-in-law, her sister Betsey's husband. He's young and handsome and, like the rest of their family, comes from Louisiana. I have to say that if he preached near where I lived, I'd be there every week. What he said was heart-warming, funny and loving. And the whole time I was weeping like a fool.

Jack wore a blue suit with white Converse trainers – a step up from his original choice of footwear, Birkenstocks – as did his best man Jamie, whose friendship, as Jack described it on the day, was 'mostly aided by the amount of time we stood together outside the headmaster's office'.

Lisa looked like a fairy princess in a white silk gown with a full skirt of billowing white tulle. Her hand-stitched veil cascaded down her back in fabulous contrast to her rich, dark hair, which was beautifully styled in a chic bob. Unlike so many people who get married with some fucking cottage loaf on their heads then regret it every time they look at their wedding photos, she had wisely kept her look natural. But then she's a model and an actress, so she knows what suits her.

And little Pearly Queen, our darling baby granddaughter, looked utterly edible in a cream dress, teensy-weensy white sandals and a cute lace 'tiara' perched on her then hairless head.

They exchanged rings, both engraved inside with the words *You are all I see* from their favourite song, Queen's 'You're My Best Friend'. That said it all about these two. Yes, they're deeply in love, but they are also great mates who watch out for each other. As Lisa said at the time, they had already been through a lifetime's worth of problems in the previous year, so you just know that they have what it takes to endure.

There was one guest who failed to enter into the spirit of the occasion. Here we were, in this tropical idyll, yet the groom's father was being snappy and sarcastic. And not just with me: it was with pretty much everyone.

With our families coming together, there were guests who, at the beginning, we didn't know well or even at all. So I found myself overcompensating for Ozzy's behaviour by laughing hysterically at anything anyone said in a bid to cover up the fact that he was being such an unpleasant shit. I didn't confront him because I didn't want to provoke something even worse. It would only have been the more acutely embarrassing for everyone. I understood that social functions like weddings are hard for alcoholics, because they have to sit there with a glass of juice or water in their hands while everyone else knocks back wine and cocktails. So I put his irritability down to that.

He was fine with Jack and Lisa themselves. Even *he* couldn't be such an arse that he'd spoil his own son's wedding with his moody shit – but, at best, he was still remote, slightly removed from the occasion, just not connecting. If I found myself anywhere near him, I felt my body tense up, so I kept out of his way as much as possible. I have never been much good at hiding my emotions, and after the ceremony was over and my new daughter-in-law came over to hug me, I knew that my eyes were puffed and blotchy, and when we pulled apart, she looked perplexed.

'I just have to ask . . . are these tears of joy, or tears of sorrow?'

'Joy,' I smiled, but the truth was that it was a bit of

both. Happiness at their marriage, sadness at the state of Ozzy's and mine. It should have been one of the happiest days of our lives; instead, we sleepwalked through it like two strangers.

As a special wedding memento, we had bought Jack a Tiffany watch and Lisa a gold Tiffany locket. Correction; *I* had bought them and added Ozzy's name to the card. He was so detached at the time that if you asked him now what we'd bought, he wouldn't have a clue.

It's funny, we all grow up witnessing the pattern of our parents' behaviour towards each other, and some of us repeat it whether we want to or not and some of us kick against it and plough a new furrow for ourselves. Jack is the latter. And he has married a woman who is beautiful on the inside and the outside, someone who comes from a normal, loving family and is calm personified.

He and Lisa are so mature, measured and sensible that I am in complete awe of them. Their obvious compatibility and happiness makes me emotional every time I think about it.

At the start of the ceremony, Jack faced Lisa and read out a speech.

'I promise to always take care of you the way you take care of me. I will always do my best to be a good husband and father, no matter what. You are my best friend, the mother of my child, and I'm very excited that, in a few minutes, you're going to be my wife.'

For the umpteenth time since we'd flown in from LA, I glanced sideways at my husband and wondered what he was thinking, whether the solid message – that love is a decision, not just a feeling – had sunk in. But he was just staring straight ahead at the happy couple, his face betraying nothing.

Night descends swiftly in Hawaii, and before we knew it, it was dark and time for a celebratory supper illuminated by table candles and those tall tiki torches. We ate traditional Hawaiian fare: grilled local fish, Lilikoi ribs, teriyaki-glazed steaks and tropical fruit. Jamie made a speech that he said had been tricky to write because, as Jack had been sober for so long, 'he has more stories to tell about me than I do about him'.

Then it was Kelly's turn. We all expected something quirky and outlandish, but she kept it simple and heartfelt.

'Jack, I am so unbelievably proud of you, of the man you have become . . . even though I am your older sister, I am pretty much the younger sister because you are a lot cleverer than me, a lot smarter and a lot more put-together than I am. I love you and Lisa so much.'

My speech was a short one, but said it all. I told Jack that I couldn't have asked for a better son and that I had learnt so much from him.

Ozzy did not want to be involved and, once the dancing started, he left. He didn't dance with the new bride, the bride's mother, or his wife of thirty years. He just buggered off, the first one to leave. The evening ended with the young people back on the beach, laughing and chatting. For a while I joined them, but then thought, No. This is the time for Jack to be with his friends, so I left and went to bed.

The next morning we had a buffet-style brunch. Everyone was relaxed, talking about the previous day's festivities. Nobody had to struggle for conversation. It was just so lovely and natural, with Pearl being carried from table to table. It had been a long way from Louisiana, but Lisa's family had fallen in love with Hawaii. They left determined to come back. In fact,

Lisa's sister Betsey and brother-in-law Ryan – the preacher who married them – are now thinking of moving there.

While the wedding was over, the festivities were not. The next day was my sixtieth birthday and I had asked all the close friends and family who'd come for the ceremony to stay. Gloria was there with Geezer, and Colin Newman and his wife Mette. Gina had to get special permission to take Olly and Amelia out of school. And Melinda, the nanny when we were filming *The Osbournes*, came with her children from Australia. And of course there were Aimee, Kelly, Jack, Lisa and Pearl. I thought it was time we got out on to that sparkling sea. So I'd chartered a boat to take us around the coast to where there's a monument to the great navigator, Captain Cook, who mapped the South Pacific and discovered Australia and who was murdered when he came back unexpectedly to Hawaii. Once we got there, we all went snorkelling, even Ozzy.

The one person who hadn't been looking forward to this sea excursion was Colin, who always gets seasick. But as a gesture of friendship and of the occasion, he agreed to come. Big mistake. There's always a bit of a roll on the Pacific. He was standing next to Gloria, Geezer and me at the rail, just chatting, when suddenly his head slumped on to Geezer's shoulder, his eyes rolled into his head and his stomach began visibly to undulate, like a belly dancer's, or as if an alien was about to pop out. My first thought was that he had had a stroke. Ozzy thought it was epilepsy and started slapping his face, then Jack started screaming at his father because he was hitting Colin, and I was screaming because that's what I do when I panic. It was like something out of a comedy skit.

We immediately turned the boat round and headed back. Three other sailors offered to bail with Colin and took him back to the hotel to sleep it off. Mette had seen it all before and knew it wasn't serious, so she stayed with us. 'I'm not wasting a great day like this in a darkened hotel room,' she said. As she predicted, Colin was fine. It was just a violent attack of seasickness. And it *was* a great day, perhaps the best birthday I think I've ever had. What could have been nicer than to spend the day with friends and family? We had sailed on an azure sea, had a picnic lunch on a South Sea island beach and had the fun of snorkelling among tropical fish. We'd even had comedy and drama.

And for once, Ozzy was even pleasant, though – as usual – he failed to give me a present. I told people he'd bought me a Richard Avedon photograph, but the truth was that I'd bought it for myself.

14

Hell with Chandeliers

It was getting harder to hide the fact that my marriage
was now in serious trouble.

Back in LA, life's rhythm returned to something like normal. Ozzy was now in Malibu, recording with the band. I was back at *The Talk*. Jack was getting on with his life, as were Kelly and Aimee. They were all living in their own places, doing their own thing. They were always trying to involve me, but I often felt like an encumbrance. I wanted to be a parent they came to see when they *wanted* to, not one they fretted about.

As usual, we tried to have Sunday lunch together whenever we could, but I knew the hurdle of Christmas was looming. Although I love the run-up and all the preparations, Christmas is always a hard time in our house, and always has been, largely because of alcohol.

———

Unbreakable

More than any other season, it's the time of year which revolves around drink, from chocolate liqueurs to rum punch to Santa's sherry and brandy butter – the entire period is soaked in booze. Recovering alcoholics are always reminding each other that Christmas Day is 25 December and that's all. But AA are the first to recognise that Christmas is a particularly vulnerable time – and in large cities there are marathons, meetings that run from lunchtime on Christmas Eve right through to Boxing Day, where you can have a cup of tea or just be with people who know you're not feeling great. Alcoholics are often estranged from their families. The rest of the year they learn to cope, helped by regular meetings and by their sponsors and sober coaches, but at Christmas there's often no escape. Finding yourself alone – knowing your children are opening their presents without you – is very hard. But if you're allowed back, then alcohol will always be around and often in liberal quantities, festive packs of beer stacked up in the fridge being the least of it. In every house you go to there'll be bottles of bubbly on the go, half-glasses of this and that will be littering the place, abandoned on the hall table, on mantelpieces, on the cistern when you go for a piss. This is temptation at its most biblical.

Given Ozzy's recent volatile moods, I was feeling particularly apprehensive. Once children leave home, you can't count on them to be around for Christmas. Kelly had already told me she was going to be spending the holiday with her boyfriend Matt's family in Detroit. So that was going to feel weird anyway. And Lisa's parents were coming up from Louisiana to spend Christmas with the new little family. We would see Jack, of course, but it would be different. The plan was that Ozzy and I would spend Christmas morning at their house for a late brunch, so that both sets of grandparents could enjoy Pearl opening up her first Christmas gifts.

And that's what happened. When we got there, it was a hive of activity: kids running around, food being prepared, family everywhere. It was exactly as a happy house should be at Christmas: warm, inviting, festooned with decorations. At the heart of it all was our gorgeous little granddaughter, who was inevitably the centre of attention. Ozzy tried as best he could to socialise, but I could see it was a struggle. He was completely detached from the rest of us, smiling when required but seemingly not spontaneously or genuinely. He was very, very quiet.

We left Jack's house at around 4 p.m. and went back to Walden Drive, where I had arranged a traditional Christmas dinner for a few friends. Aimee would be the only one of our children celebrating with us this year, and she too had invited a couple of friends. I had also invited Gloria and Geezer and Belle Zwerdling, plus an interior designer friend called Martyn Laurence-Ballard. Then Aimee called me to say that she wasn't up to coming. She was running a temperature and thought she'd probably got the tummy bug which was doing the rounds in LA that winter, a twenty-four-hour gastric flu.

The evening was fine. Very low-key, which was exactly what I needed. We had our English Christmas dinner with turkey, roast potatoes, Brussels sprouts, bread sauce, the lot. Even plum pudding. But when everyone had gone, and I'd finished pottering around in the kitchen, Ozzy disappeared again, cutting himself off from me. In the old days we'd have had a chat, talked about what was said, all the usual things couples do when they've had friends in. I found him in the living room with the curtains pulled tight, the television blaring, just like he was most days, even when it was bright sunshine outside.

He had been fine about going to Jack and Lisa's, but other than that, he didn't want to go anywhere. He would complain bitterly if I even mentioned going out, acting short-tempered and nasty, trying to belittle me by saying that I would go to the opening of an envelope when all I was actually suggesting was a supper with some friends. I now knew what people meant when they referred to their marriage feeling like two strangers living under the same roof. The situation was becoming impossible.

Despite his animosity towards me, we were still sleeping in the same bed. If I haven't flounced off to a hotel and we are actually under the same roof, I have always stayed in the marital bed come hell or high water. I have always felt that if we started to occupy separate bedrooms, it would stay that way permanently and there would be no going back.

A couple of weeks after the tricky Christmas, we were fast asleep, having both taken a sleeping pill. I take them sporadically, usually when I have a lot on my mind, but Ozzy has to take one every night or he'd be pacing the floor like a wide-eyed lunatic. Presumably, because his body is so used to them, the tablets don't put him into such a deep sleep as they do me, though he claims I could be in an actual coma and still take a phone call. But this particular night I heard the sound of something like glass breaking, and it had stirred me. I ignored it and tried to go back to sleep. It was he who woke up at 3.30 a.m. to find the bedroom filled with smoke.

'Shaaaaaaaron! The fucking house is on fire!'

That woke me up. I leapt out of bed, ran for where I thought the door was and crashed straight into Ozzy, who was panicking like a headless chicken because he couldn't see anything.

To add to the comedic element, he had just had a small operation to try and alleviate a spot of arthritis in his right hand and, although we thought it was only a minor procedure, it actually took two hours and he had come home with his arm fully plastered at right angles to his body, his forearm raised and a splint structure connecting it to his neck. He looked like a fucking deranged air-traffic controller.

As I went around opening doors and windows, which Ozzy later claimed only exacerbated the fire, he headed off to the living room to find the wooden coffee table ablaze.

Ask Ozzy about 'the candle fire' and he'll reply, '*Which* fucking candle fire? We've had loads.'

In reality, we have only had a couple, both at Welders in England, and this one in LA was, ahem, *only* the third. My problem is that I love candles. Every house I have ever lived in has looked like a church on All Saints Day. They're everywhere – on every table, shelf, mantelpiece and in the downstairs loo. But occasionally, I forget to blow one of them out.

The guilty candle on this occasion was a Christmas present from my former *America's Got Talent* co-host Howard Stern. It had burned so low that the glass had shattered and the naked flame had caught the coffee table, which now resembled a bonfire in the middle of the room.

We rang the fire brigade but, in the meantime, tried to put the fire out ourselves. Ozzy went to fetch a wet towel to throw over it, and I returned from the kitchen bearing a saucepan of water. But as I threw it, it seemed to push the flames towards Ozzy and suddenly his arm was on fire. Thankfully he managed to pat it out straight away, but his plaster was left slightly charred.

As the house was still full of smoke, we went out into the front garden to wait for the firemen. So there we were, surrounded by a menagerie of dogs, when the fire engine arrived.

'Has someone here reported a fire?' the first one asked.

'No, I always sit in the garden fucking smouldering,' said Ozzy.

Dramas over, I returned to *The Talk* and carried on with my other job of managing Ozzy's career. For three years we'd been working on making a movie out of Ozzy's autobiography and, as ever with the film industry, it was taking an age to find the financing, the right writer, and so on. Then, one of the people we were working with on developing it said they had found the perfect writer and could Ozzy and I fly to England in February to meet him? 'Consider it done,' I said, 'we're there.'

The timing was perfect, as Ozzy and I had been asked

to present at the Brits. Also, I'd been asked by Richard Curtis, the founder of Comic Relief, if I'd be interested in doing a sketch. I have loved David Walliams ever since seeing *Little Britain* all those years ago. So this sounded like just what the doctor ordered. I said yes straight away. I took a week off from *The Talk* and we flew to England.

While I was busy filming in a church in Hampshire, Ozzy met up with the writer and they bonded. It finally started to look like the movie was becoming a reality, and his mood was upbeat.

Unfortunately the tight schedule meant that I had to abandon him at Heathrow the moment we landed at around 11 a.m. And that's all part of the problem: Ozzy and I are always fighting time. So that didn't go down too well.

Two days later we were due to present the award for International Best Female Solo Artist at the Brits, but on the morning of the show he said, 'I'm not fucking doing it.' So, fine. So much for raising his profile a few weeks before the release of *13*. It didn't matter; I ended up presenting it with *X Factor* host Dermot O'Leary. I simply left my miserable husband at home, muttering to himself about 'Mrs Fucking TV', which was his new term of abuse.

When we're over in England we always stay at Welders, if humanly possible. It's the loveliest house, set in acres of beautiful rolling hills. Incredibly, it's not even an hour's drive from the centre of London. It's our home. The plan had always been that we would stay for eight days and then fly back to LA. The main reason was *The Talk*. I'd been given a week off, but that was it. Afterwards, I had to go back to work.

Two days before we were due to leave, Ozzy blows a gasket.

'I'm not coming.'

'What do you mean, you're not coming?'

'I'm not fucking coming.'

He then comes out with the usual spiel: 'I'm fed up of travelling. I never spend enough time at Welders.' All of which was true.

As he was scheduled to be back in England three weeks later to do a lot of press for the Sabbath album – interviews for magazines which have long lead times – he didn't see the point of coming back with me now just to turn round again in three weeks. All the reasons he gave for not going back were perfectly reasonable. But he didn't argue reasonably or coherently. He just went on and on about it. Finally I told him, 'You do what you want. I have commitments in LA, I have to return.'

And then it really kicked off.

'I fucking hate you.'

'Sorry?'

'I *said*, I fucking hate you.'

Right. Here we go again, I thought. Back on the bloody roller-coaster.

I knew he had just employed the oldest trick in the book: start an argument so you can flounce off and do what you want. But I was too tired to fight it. Besides, I had commitments and contracts to uphold, so I *had* to go back.

So he stayed behind, poncing about in his Audi R8 convertible that he kept at Welders, and I left for the States wondering what the hell was going to happen next. It didn't take long for me to find out. A lovely couple called Dave and Sharon run the house for us in the UK. They've been working for us for at least ten years and they know Ozzy of old. After a couple of days, Dave rang and told me that Ozzy was behaving so unpredictably that it was like 'having the Exorcist in the house'. Not a lot I could do.

Then, one week in, I got an email from Ozzy to say that he was going away for a couple of days to try and 'find' himself. I resisted the temptation to reply that he should start by looking up his own arse.

People have the impression, I'm told, that Ozzy is a technophobe. Nonsense. Ozzy can email, Skype, text, you name it. He's perfectly competent at new technology if he wants to be. I called the house and, by some miracle, he answered. He said, 'Hello,' but anything beyond that was like getting blood from a stone. He was sullen and wholly uncommunicative, but even I couldn't have predicted what came next.

'I think I need to be a bachelor.'

'Whaaaat? A bachelor? Have you heard yourself? You're a fucking *pensioner*. You need a bus pass, that's what you need.'

I slammed the phone down and stared into space for a while, wondering what on earth was going on inside my husband's head. Was this just a classic mid-life crisis? He'd always had long hair and a penchant for rock music, so they couldn't be classed as defining features, but the sports cars were a new development – the Audi R8 and *two* fucking Ferraris lying idle in LA – and so too was this recent Greta Garbo 'I vont to be alone' bollocks.

Later in the day, I called the house again and this time, Dave answered. He said that Ozzy had gone out hours earlier and had not yet returned home. Worse, he'd taken the car.

That frightened me, the thought of him driving back drunk. I wasn't worried for him, but for everybody else; because invariably the fuckers who drive drunk don't get hurt themselves, they just hurt other people. I was fuming. *Fuming.* I felt impotent, stuck in LA, but sent Dave and his wife Sharon driving round Buckinghamshire to look for him. Eventually, they saw the car parked outside a pub, and tucked under the windscreen wiper was a note from a dealer offering to get him drugs! Beyond pathetic.

So Dave went inside the pub and Ozzy was just sitting there, drinking God knows what, and he refused to come home. Dave made an effort to persuade him, but Ozzy tried to start a fight so he backed off and left him. And all this time I was at my wit's end in Beverly

Hills, getting updates on my husband's drunken idiocy and feeling completely helpless to do anything about it.

He must have slept in the car, because he arrived back at the house the next day carrying a bottle of vodka and a crate of beer. By now it had been established that he'd drunk our garage dry. There was no alcohol in the main house, but in the garage there were a few bits and pieces like old Christmas hampers people had sent us. God knows how long they'd been there, but he'd worked his way through every drop of alcohol he could find.

Everything fell into place. The arsehole behaviour at Jack and Lisa's wedding; the same crap over most of Christmas. Just as, earlier, I had thought it might be, I now knew for sure. He was begrudging every drink that anyone took and every laugh that anyone had because he was craving alcohol and was unhappy with himself. The hostility finally made sense: it was his guilt, his anger at himself for being so weak.

I called Dave again.

'Get his car removed from the house. In fact, take *every* car away. I'm going to sell every last fucking one of them.'

Within twenty-four hours, I had sold the Audi R8 in England and one of the Ferraris he kept in America. The other one went to Jack. All gone. There was no way I was going to risk him getting in one of them while he was drunk and hurting someone.

Ozzy says now that it proved to be the most expensive drink he's ever had, but at the time he was none the wiser because I had stopped talking to him. The way I felt, he could have stayed in England for good and drunk himself to death.

Then the text came.

'I need help. I'm hurting. I've been using for a year and a half.'

And that was it. I knew he had reached probably one of the lowest points that addicts have to hit before they finally accept that they need help. I also know, from my years of experience with it, that *until* that acceptance hits them, there's not a damn thing anyone else can do to make them get sober.

A friend of ours, Billy Morrison, who has been in the programme for years, flew to England to collect him. But Ozzy was in no fit state to fly. He was screaming for help. Quite apart from having the shakes, he had a terrible stabbing pain in his chest and didn't know why. He just woke up with it one morning after blanking out on booze, just like the bad old days.

Billy took him to the doctor's. His blood pressure was totally through the roof and an X-ray showed that he'd broken his sternum, but to this day he doesn't know how he did it. Add to this the fact that he was detoxing, and you get the picture. It was eight days before he was considered well enough to board a plane back to LA.

As luck would have it, I had just sold our house in Hidden Hills to singer and actress Jessica Simpson. The downside was that I had to pack up 13,500 square foot of house in a matter of weeks. Jessica wanted to move in within the month. I was in the middle of packing when Ozzy returned with Billy. Talk about stressful. I had moved out of the rented house on Walden Drive and taken my stuff to the Beverly Hills Hotel. Every afternoon, once *The Talk* was over, it was back to Hidden Hills with the packers, trying to get out in time. I'd made up my mind. There was no way I was going to be in the same house as Ozzy this time, playing happy families. I was furious with him for taking the second chance I had given him and throwing it back in my face. He had betrayed my trust, but worse, he was failing as a father and now a grandfather. It was time, I felt, for him to grow up.

I knew he would be staying at Walden Drive, which I was constantly referring to as the Dark House. I had come to loathe it there. Its gloominess made me feel stifled, as if my throat was constricted. Every time I pulled on to the driveway and then on through the small tunnel that led to the front of the house, I felt a sense of impending doom. The dark wooden floors and panelling that I had always been fond of now felt crushing and life-sapping to me. I needed somewhere light and spacious to live. No more dungeons.

I thought back to the previous July, how Ozzy had promised he was going to work a rigid programme of sobriety, how sorry he was, asking for forgiveness. To think I'd actually believed him! It was nothing more than the usual bullshit. I couldn't bear to think that he was back to square one; same old shit, just a different day.

At Walden Drive, Billy Morrison was trying to work

out a rigid programme for Ozzy. This would involve attending at least one AA meeting a day, maybe two. Sometime earlier, we had arranged for Jack to go to Germany for treatment for his MS. Originally, Ozzy was supposed to be coming, but the last thing Jack needed was his father ricocheting around the clinic going cold turkey from drugs and alcohol, so we left him behind at the Dark House where, as far as I was concerned, he could stew in his own juice. Having Ozzy along was never an option at this point.

In retrospect, perhaps Jack's having MS, and his courage in fighting it, strengthened my resolve in staying away from Ozzy for far longer than I might normally have done. When one of your children is sick or given a potentially life-threatening diagnosis, everything else diminishes in importance. I loved Ozzy as much as I had always done, but this time, *his* illness seemed somehow pathetic compared to our son's. It was something I just didn't have the inclination or the time to focus on. There were bigger issues at play.

In February 2013, right after Ozzy had been rescued from himself at Welders and brought back to LA a jabbering wreck by Billy, Jack, Lisa and I headed off

My precious granddaughter Pearl.

Clockwise from top left: Pearl with her daddy and aunt Kelly; Pearl models a Sabbath T-shirt with granddad; with Lisa, truly one of the family; Pearl checking out her reflection; ladies who lunch (centre).

The whole family was devastated by Jack's MS diagnosis, but his response has been truly inspiring. Here he is receiving the Medal of Hope award for his charity work at the 2013 Race to Erase MS gala.

At the Race to Erase MS event with Lisa, Jack, our good friend Nancy Davis and Kelly.

The story of a marriage.

1982

2007

2013

Moving out and moving on. The picture that revealed to the world that mine and Ozzy's marriage was really on the rocks this time.

Meanwhile, Ozzy was celebrating the success of Sabbath's reunion album, *13*, which went to number 1 in the UK and around the world.

Appearing in this sketch with Olly Murs, Louis Walsh, Simon Cowell, David Walliams and Dermot O'Leary was, quite literally, Comic Relief after my recent troubles.

At dinner in London with Simon, Louis and Sinitta, after we wrapped filming the Comic Relief sketch.

Guess who's back?

With Louis, Nicole Scherzinger and Gary Barlow for series 10 of *The X Factor*. This time around it's all genuine laughter and friendship.

The Osbournes. Everything I do has always been for Jack, Ozzy, Kelly and Aimee.

With my husband and best friend Ozzy at the Daytime Emmy Awards in June 2013.

to the Infusio Center for New Medicine in Frankfurt, Germany.

We had been told about a revolutionary stem-cell treatment that isn't allowed in the States because it hasn't been trialled for long enough, and its efficacy has not yet been fully evaluated. But as far as we could tell, the worst thing that could happen would be nothing.

Jack said that his philosophy was to take a 360-degree approach to his MS to maximise his chances of thwarting its symptoms. A balanced diet, keep fit, sleep well, positive thinking, that kind of thing. And the stem-cell treatment was part of that overview. We knew that the treatment wouldn't cure Jack's MS, but the best-case scenario was that it would possibly help his body to repair some of the existing damage and build up his immune system to make him as healthy as he could be to fight the onset of the disease.

The clinic describes stem cells as life's 'library' and 'construction workers', responsible for the renewal and healing of the entire body. They harvest them from bone marrow or, in my and Jack's case, from about 300 cc of circulating blood that was taken once we had arrived at the clinic. They sorted the cells and checked them for quality, then incubated them with cytokines (cell-signalling molecules) to stimulate replication. About a week later, they had enough stem cells for implantation and injected them into our lymphatic system. The idea was that those new cells would then utilise the rest to rejuvenate necrotic and damaged tissue and, in an ideal world, bring the body's healing elements into play to fix what was wrong. Depending on your age and fitness, they can get something like 800,000 to nearly two million stem cells that way.

When Jack's results came back, they were excellent. He was in the top group of yield because of his youth and fitness. My yield was pretty lousy because of our age difference and, presumably, the damage done not only by my ill health but also from all the unnecessary procedures I had put my body through. But we were really happy about Jack's results.

I texted Ozzy to let him know, but we didn't actually speak. This was all about Jack, and I had no appetite for dealing with anyone else's problems.

Did the stem-cell therapy work? I really don't know,

but it certainly doesn't do any harm and Jack has now dropped a load of weight and is feeling pretty good, so fingers crossed. You have to have it done every two years. It's not a cure, they're not saying that. But if it gets his immune system in top order, then it might stall an outbreak or even stop it from happening.

For now, that's all we can hope for.

It was about five weeks since I had last seen Ozzy, just before I left him in England. I was now back in LA, so I texted him to say I wanted to meet up. Obviously I was interested in the state of mind he was in. I wanted to have a plan of where we were going from here.

It was a Sunday morning, and he came from Walden Drive to my hotel room. He was all dressed up in a suit and the usual array of gothic jewellery, so I took this as a good sign, that perhaps he had made a special effort because he wanted to look nice for me. But as soon as he opened his mouth, he was cocky, his tone arrogant. There didn't seem to be one shred of remorse at his behaviour; there was no apology forthcoming. His tone was cold, his attitude along the lines of, so, what do you want to do then?

Something snapped. I thought, I can't carry his shit any more. It's what I have always done, and I'm tired.

'I want a divorce.'

'You're not *serious*.'

He didn't look shocked. I don't think he believed me but, at the time, I meant it wholeheartedly.

I was expecting him to be mortified and remorseful, begging me to take him back, but his reply was said with something like a sneer.

'I am. I want half of everything, that's my right. And I also want a hundred grand a month.'

I knew that money was Ozzy's Achilles heel, and that the thought of losing it might have more impact than the thought of losing me.

'No fucking way. Over my dead body.'

My Achilles heel is respect, namely the lack of it in other people, and I felt he was being dismissive, so that was it. Snap. I was drinking a cappuccino at the time and the whole lot went on his head. The coffee, the cup *and* the bloody saucer. Then I grabbed him and pulled at his precious hair with one hand, while trying to yank off his jewellery with the other.

He went for me, trying to grab me in a headlock. We

must have made quite a noise because Ozzy's assistant, Big Dave, came rushing in and placed himself between us, holding me back and pushing Ozzy away.

After Dave took Ozzy out of the room, I was physically and mentally exhausted.

There were a couple of very formal texts that went back and forth, mostly to do with work or the kids because he was still in regular contact with them. Whatever was going on with Ozzy and me at the time, it never affected the kids' attitudes towards their dad.

But other than that, there was no communication between us. The man I had been with, or had spoken to pretty much every day for the past three decades, suddenly felt like a stranger to me. Was this how it was going to end after we'd been through so much together?

The kids kept asking me what was going on. They had grown used to our arguments over the years, but us living apart from each other was something new that they couldn't quite comprehend.

It was all, 'But, Mum, it's not *really* serious, is it? You'll sort it out soon, won't you?' They understood why I needed to be away from their father, but at the same time our marriage, however turbulent it had always been, was their normality. It was all they had ever known, so for us to be living apart was very disturbing for them, even though they were now adults themselves.

I didn't tell them too much about what was swirling around inside my head, or relay the level of my anger at Ozzy. I wanted to keep them out of it as best I could. For me, there were no sides; it wasn't the school playground. Sometimes, Ozzy would leave a message with one of them for me, and I would tell them, 'Say hi to Dad, I hope he's doing good.'

Hidden Hills was now gone: sold and emptied, gone. Ozzy was living in the Dark House in Walden Drive. I was in a bungalow in the Beverly Hills Hotel. Not having a place you can truly call your own is very unsettling, even if everything else is fine. Then a house came on the market that I happened to know very well, of which I had very happy memories, something that I could have done with now.

When I moved to Los Angeles in 1976, I had made friends with an elderly couple called Gert and Sonny Silverstein. Gert was an interior designer and antiques dealer, and she had worked on the house I moved into.

We had hit it off from the start, and I used to spend day after day at their house on North Crescent Drive, a few doors down from the Beverly Hills Hotel where I was staying until my place was ready. Their house felt like a second home to me. I absolutely adored them, and they adored me.

Gert and Sonny are both dead now, God rest their souls. After they passed – about twelve years ago – their house was sold. But now I saw that it was back on the market. The asking price was way too high, but I kept my eye on it. And when it didn't sell, I enquired about renting and secured a two-year deal from March 2013. It was years since I'd seen it, and as I wandered round I realised that there was quite a lot to be done to make it feel like home. An Osbourne house needs lots of televisions and gadgets, acres of hanging and shelf space for clothes and plenty of chandeliers, the more the merrier.

If I'd owned it, I would have gutted most of the rooms and started again, but as I was only renting, that wasn't an option. It would be a case of tweaking around the edges. In the meantime, I would continue to live at the hotel. So now I was responsible for two houses, North Crescent Drive and Walden Drive. All the while

I was living out of a couple of suitcases. I remember sitting in the Beverly Hills Hotel one night, on my own, and thinking, Oh, for fuck's sake, my entire life is in a bloody box and I don't know where anything is. It was not a happy time.

I'd get up each morning, go to work at *The Talk*, then come back to the hotel and just take to my bed. I'd make a few imperative phone calls, often to do with Black Sabbath business, then pull the duvet over my head and sleep for the rest of the day. Sleep, sleep, sleep. It felt like I was shutting down.

I was in a pretty bad way, to be honest, in a state of permanent exhaustion. I only needed a couple of glasses of wine and then I'd be fast asleep. But then the sober light of day would come round again, and I would feel physically sick. I felt constantly as if I wanted to throw up, that doing so might get rid of the tight knot in my stomach, but I never could. That feeling never went away; it just got bigger and bigger. It was a physical pain from feeling so hurt.

I thought I knew Ozzy so well that I could virtually predict what his next thought or move would be, and then there I was, thinking, Oh my God, I don't know this man, I don't know *anything* about him. It was just a huge shock, that he'd given me a load of bullshit and I'd been pulled in. Now I couldn't find two shoes that fucking matched, the dogs were all over the place and God knew what was going on inside my husband's head. Our life had been shattered to pieces by his behaviour, and I couldn't believe that it had come to this. I had invested thirty-three years of my life in him, our family, what we stood for . . . and where had it left me? Alone in a hotel room in my pyjamas at three in the afternoon.

Ozzy and I had communicated occasionally via text and, although I was keeping busy, I was still going over and over everything constantly in my mind. I'd wake up each morning, spend a few seconds staring into the darkness as I tried to work out where the hell I was and then, after that microscopic spell of blissful ignorance, my brain would fill up with all the crap going on with Ozzy.

Even though he was at Walden Drive, just a few blocks away, I kept my distance. I never went there unless I was sure he was somewhere else. After the showdown the previous July, when he'd promised to stay sober, I didn't trust him not to betray me again. But there was no game plan in my head about what to do. The state I was in, I was lucky to be functioning at all.

For the first time ever, I removed my wedding ring. For me, this was a massively significant thing to do, but I just didn't feel connected to him so I didn't want to wear it. On 14 April, I was photographed without it while helping to unload a removal van delivering my belongings to the North Crescent Drive house, so of course that sparked even more fevered speculation in the press about the state of our marriage.

Inevitably, it started to leak out that we were possibly living apart, particularly as an agency reporter had been tailing us. You didn't have to be Sherlock bloody Holmes to suss out quite quickly that we weren't being seen together and were travelling to separate houses.

Once the rumours started appearing in newspapers and on websites, friends began calling to ask if everything was all right, and I was having questions fired at me by reporters wherever I went. We live in this instant world now, where everything you wear, say or do can be on the internet within seconds, and it's really disconcerting. It's constant, constant, constant, and everybody is out to make a buck by selling a picture of you, however shit it is.

I was still Ozzy's manager and having to work on the tour and the album. We never met face to face, but every day there was another conference call or another meeting, so suddenly he would be there, in front of me, while I was trying desperately hard just to keep it professional and not burst into tears.

Usually I'm quite good at keeping emotional matters separate from business, but this time I struggled. I did the vital stuff, dealing with other people and overseeing contractual issues, but when it came to being somewhere just as background support, I began to bow out. As work started to crank up around the album, I didn't even go to the listening party for the press because I just didn't think it was fair to bring the bad atmosphere between me and Ozzy to the other guys in the band. I wouldn't have been able to hide it, so I thought it best to stay away. It was their time, not mine, and needless to say, Ozzy didn't ring to find out why I wasn't there.

I was just trying to find the strength to keep walking.

The moment the Black Sabbath album went to number one in America should have been a defining moment for me as well as for Ozzy, a time of supreme celebration. I had worked my butt off to help get it there, for years and years. But I was numb. Just numb.

The new house was sitting there, ready for me to move into, but I felt so overwhelmed by it. My entire life was there, all sixty years of it, in boxes, everything I had. But every time I went there, I couldn't cope. I would walk in the front door, take a look round, then run off back to the hotel and hide. I would literally pull the sheets over my head thinking, I can't do this. And so it went on, week after week. I just couldn't get myself together. I didn't know where to begin. I didn't *want* to begin.

Meanwhile, Sabbath were off touring Australia and New Zealand, and I decided to take a long weekend away and flew to Mexico with Aimee and her boyfriend Michael. I just needed to get away, and thought that a change of scene might make me feel better about my life. How wrong I was.

It was just my luck that someone recognised me at once. The very next morning after I got there the place was surrounded by paparazzi. Someone had sold the story to a Belfast newspaper, and once it was out that I was staying there, photographers pursued us everywhere we went, even during a day trip on a boat. There are pictures of me looking suicidal, as if I'm about to chuck myself over the side and be done with it. But actually I was deep in thought, mulling over my problems and wondering what to do next. I didn't feel settled anywhere, I just felt lost. I might as well have stayed at the bloody hotel in LA.

Straight after the second relapse, I had said to Ozzy that it was going to take at least a year of sobriety on his part to get us back together. I told him it had to be an AA meeting a day, working the steps religiously and a full commitment to staying clean and sober. You can't just say, OK, I'm fine now; you have to work at it over a long period of time.

But I missed my old life, I missed *him*. I wanted him back. So it became my mission to make him see what he had in life and, more importantly, what he could lose. I wanted him to look at everything he had worked for, and what he was throwing away because of the fucking drink and drugs. I wanted to scream at him, 'Are you fucking *mad*? Are you so juvenile that you can't get a handle on your behaviour?'

The pictures of me staring out to sea in Mexico went global. Ozzy was in Australia when he saw them, and the very next day he put a letter on his Facebook page, an open letter which read:

For the last year and a half I have been drinking and taking drugs. I was in a very dark place and was an asshole to the people I love most, my family. However, I am happy to say that I am now 44 days sober. Just to set the record straight, Sharon and I are not divorcing. I'm just trying to be a better person. I would like to apologise to Sharon, my family, my friends and my bandmates for my insane behaviour during this period . . . and my fans. God bless, Ozzy

The next morning I woke up to Ozzy's statement. I was stunned. After reading it, I realised he had come a very long way in the forty-four days he'd been sober. I admired his honesty, and truly felt that he wanted his family back. And where he said he was trying to be a better person, I was a hundred per cent sure that he was trying. So I texted him and told him how proud I was of him, and how brave I thought he'd been.

His response was, 'I'm honestly trying, and I love you.'

I returned to *The Talk* on the Monday. Now it was all very public.

Up until Ozzy's statement, I hadn't commented on my personal situation other than to my family and close friends. However, my co-hosts on *The Talk* knew what was going on, but had very kindly desisted from asking me to speak about it on air. But now it was out there, in black and white on Ozzy's Facebook page, I knew I had to say something.

'It's our business and we're dealing with it,' I told the viewers. 'We're not getting divorced. However, am I happy? No. Am I upset? Yes, I am – I'm devastated right now.'

I said that Ozzy was in a very dark place, that his disease didn't just hurt him but his family too, and that we had been through worse and would cope with it.

'Otherwise my husband will be taken to the hospital to get my foot removed from his ass,' I quipped. But off air I was, at best, morose; at worst, constantly tearful.

At this point in my life I should have been at my husband's side touring in New Zealand, Australia and

Japan. But this was Black Sabbath's time to shine. I knew I wouldn't have been able to hide my emotions, so the only thing was for me to stay away. It was their moment, not mine.

People in my life were saying to me, run, run, run while you can; you can have whatever's left of your life to do what you want with, you can come and go as you please and be who you want to be. But I just couldn't. I kept on looking back at all the good times, all the connections, at the life we had made together.

The one thing I've learnt from this is, never give advice to a couple who have been together for over thirty years. Ultimately people are always going to do what they want to do. And you only end up looking like a baddie. All the well-meaning advice I'd given to friends over the years was a waste of time. First, I had no right and second, nobody else really knows what goes on between two people.

As Ozzy moved from Australia, to New Zealand, to Japan, I was still in the same bungalow at the hotel with an empty house down the road. I couldn't face opening up another box full of memories. Every time I walked through the front door, I was overwhelmed.

From the day I married Ozzy, I'd always had this thing in my mind that, if I made the perfect home, if there were flowers, if there was fruit, if I got the right bloody curtains, if it smelt lovely and looked gorgeous, then it would make everything right in our world.

He wasn't like that at all. He's always been fucking blind when it comes to the look of a place. He won't pull the chain, he won't pick clothes up from the floor, he'll eat strawberries and leave the top bits scattered all over the carpet along with cream-cracker crumbs. He's oblivious, he can't see any of it. But if there's even a tiny chink of light on the TV screen because the curtains don't close properly, he'll bloody well notice *that*. But I realised now, it wasn't Ozzy that was blind. It was me. Thinking that the perfect house equalled the perfect marriage.

I have always placed so much emphasis on the ambience of a place; I would want every house to make us happy. And if it didn't then it would be, Oh God, it's the wrong layout, the wrong location, it's too small, it's too big . . . I must sell it and *then* everything will be perfect and we'll be happy and so will the kids. But recently, after all those years of trying, of fretting about that painting ruining the room or those cushions not being plumped properly, I've realised that it means jack shit. You can't manufacture happiness.

The happiest times were when we were broke and we had nothing.

So it wasn't that the new house felt like an insurmountable interior-design project that just didn't look 'right' to move into yet. My reluctance to cross its threshold ran far deeper than that. Psychologically it was huge for me, because I was moving into somewhere on my own. The kids were grown up, with their own places, and Ozzy was living a few streets away at the Dark House. My entire life had been about making a home for them, and now it was just about me. It completely floored me. I loved this house in North Crescent Drive, and I had nothing but wonderful memories of the days I'd spent there with Gert and Sonny, but when I walked in the front door all I felt was the dull ache of loneliness.

On Ozzy's return from Japan, we decided to meet in a public place this time so that neither one of us could lose our temper. I decided on the Beverly Hills Hotel Polo Lounge. By now Ozzy was well into two months of sobriety. He had a sponsor *and* Billy Morrison was working with him as his sober coach. The sponsor works the twelve steps with you, and the sober coach is always there for you to talk to and go to meetings with. When you're as addictive as Ozzy you have to work, work, work at it. It doesn't come easily.

For the hours before we met, I had butterflies in my stomach. It seemed like for ever since I'd looked into my husband's eyes, but now I was looking into sober eyes. The man I loved was present. Remorseful. Humbled. Yet I could tell he was relieved to be sitting next to me. Just as relieved as I was to be sitting so close I could smell his cologne. I put my hand on his, took him in my arms and we both cried.

15

Addicted

The Ozzy I love.

Having read my books, readers might have formed the opinion that everything is Ozzy's fault, that I was an abused wife, someone who was so emotionally battered I couldn't see a way out of a relationship that was slowly destroying me. And yes, when Ozzy was in the dark place, back on the drink and drugs, it could sometimes feel that way. Why had I put up with all his shit over the years? Why had I tolerated his wilful absences from family life after yet another drink or drugs binge? Why had I made a stand, only to return a day or two later?

The truth is, I'm not a cowed wife; in fact, nothing could be further from the truth. Believe me, when the mood takes me I can give as good as I get, and over the years Ozzy has had to deal with the often murky complexities of *my* addictions, too. I am not an easy person to live with. I can sometimes be very selfish and manipulative. And God, I've had my issues with weight and the bulimia that goes along with it. In addition, I am a spendaholic, a spendthrift of a lifetime's standing. My relationship with money is as terrible as my father's; he didn't respect it and neither do I. For me, living life to the full has always meant spend, spend, spend.

This see-sawing behaviour has blighted my entire adult life, but only recently have I identified *another* full-on addiction: my often destructive codependency in relation to my husband.

Thinking about it now, I realise I had suspected he was using again right from the start. God knows, I had seen enough of his drug and alcohol abuse over the years to recognise the signs. But although I felt resentful towards him for this latest transgression, I also understood for the first time ever that it was partly my fault too.

I had buried any misgivings, attributing his unpleasantness towards me as stress over anything and everything except the bleedin' obvious. It was the pressure of writing the album. It was the stress of touring. It was because it was hot. It was because it was cold. It was because he was jet-lagged. It was because the dogs were being irritating. It was because he hadn't had much sleep the night before. You name it; I had the excuse for his unpleasantness. *Anything* but confront the reality.

I had turned the other cheek and *enabled* him to carry on using.

Ultimately, it was his responsibility when he went back on the drugs and alcohol, but if you read any literature on addiction, or you go to Al-Anon, the support group for relatives and friends of users, the first thing they tell you is to pack your bags and leave and don't look back. They say that tough love is the way forward because you have to make them responsible for their actions, and the only way they will work a rigid programme is if they have lost something they love through their destructive behaviour.

So at the first sign I *should* have said, 'I'm leaving.' Perhaps that might have nipped it in the bud. But I didn't. I never have. I have never put him on the spot, never made *him* responsible for his bad behaviour. I always look the other way because my attitude is, anything for a fucking peaceful life. Bury your head in the sand; tomorrow's another day and by then it will all have gone away.

Jack reckons I do it because, having seen how the break-up of Ozzy's first marriage affected his older kids, I was prepared to do whatever it took not to let that happen to *our* family; that I have a 'this too shall pass' attitude that makes me persevere through the really tough times.

There's an element of truth in that, because the residual damage of a break-up is always in the back of my mind whenever Ozzy's behaviour prompts me to think about leaving him, which is another reason we have lasted thirty years. But there are other factors at play, too.

I learnt placatory behaviour as a child because my father was so mercurial. I spent most of my formative years trying to stay on his good side and keep the peace between him and my mother so that there wouldn't be yet another ugly outburst to spoil the fragile status quo. So when I got married, it seemed only natural to carry on that pattern of behaviour.

Addicted

Ozzy could perform open-heart surgery on me without an anaesthetic and I'd tell you that he was doing it for the best. I would find every reason in the world why he could do that operation. I would actually *justify* his actions; make allowances for him in a way that I have never done or would never do for anyone else in my life. I wanted my children to have this perfect family life that I'd never had. So, to the best of my ability, I would try to keep things as harmonious as possible.

In the early days, I would sometimes try the age-old tactic of biding my time to address an issue, waiting until the atmosphere was right rather than having a reasonable chat with him there and then about how his latest bout of bad behaviour had really bothered me. The problem was, I never felt the time was right to make the point I wished to make about his most recent marital misdemeanour.

'What the fuck are you doing?' he'd fire back. 'That was yesterday. Why are you ruining a perfectly great day? You're fucking sick, you are.'

I eventually stopped saying anything, and whatever it was that had happened would never be mentioned again.

Take note that my placatory behaviour was usually for the benefit of the children when they got older, or anyone else who happened to be present, because I didn't want to pop the bubble of supposed bliss. But if he incited my anger when we were alone, God help him. I would hurt him, and he would hurt me, both physically and mentally.

It's always been one extreme or the other with me. I would either brush things under the carpet, pretending that everything in my garden was rosy when it was actually shrivelled and unattractive, or a red mist would descend and I would lash out. I have never been one of those people who can make a measured, well-articulated response. I grew up witnessing my father's violence or threatening behaviour as his solution to most problems and so, far too often, it has been a natural response for me too. I repeated the pattern. I knew I was doing it, but the difference has always been that, generally, I like people, and my father liked nobody. I respect people, he didn't.

So my pattern of behaviour in the marriage has been either placatory or pugilistic, with little in between. I have given Ozzy black eyes; I once smashed Aimee's china feeding bowl over his head when he told me he had the clap, and, more recently, there was the cup and saucer I threw at him after demanding a divorce. I'm not recounting this because I'm proud of it; most definitely not. It's just to put things in context, to illustrate that as much as Ozzy has been out of line over the years, my own behaviour hasn't exactly been exemplary.

To understand what makes us tick as a couple, you have to go back to Ozzy's childhood as well as mine. He came from a working-class family in Aston, Birmingham, and they were really good people. But you didn't have to look far back to find little formal education or experience of the world, and ancestors that were all from the workhouse.

And what was the way out for families like that? A drink, that's what. It would make them feel better. It was a laugh, a release, the same way that smoking was. It took them to another place.

Ozzy's background is getting pissed on a Friday and Saturday night, bashing the wife if she got angry with you then all sitting down for Sunday lunch as if nothing had happened before heading off to work again on the Monday morning. It was nobody's fault; it was just the hand that fate had dealt, and they were stuck in that rut. For the majority of Ozzy's generation, there was no way out of it. No way to break the mould. There weren't people around to advise and help them; they just got on with it as best they could.

Ozzy was one of the lucky few who did get out. Ozzy's escape was daydreaming that he was going to be a Beatle, or that his sister was going to marry one of the Fab Four and he could join them on the road. For him, the next best thing was to form a band with his mates, and *voilà*: the rest is heavy-metal history.

But even though he got out of Aston, the entrenched pattern of behaviour he'd learnt as a child stayed with him, as did mine. We were both working-class – though my background was more feast or famine – and we both came from families that, in different ways, were fucking nuts. But somehow we have built a life together and come out the other side of all the shit we've been through. We've invested our time, our youth, our love and our *soul* into what we have.

We all have dreams, but I have now accepted the reality: that I am married to an alcoholic and drug addict who, every single day, has to fight *not* to be that way.

Addicted

As for me, I have come to the conclusion that I am seriously workaholic. This destructive behaviour has not helped my marriage, my kids, or my health. I am like a hamster on a wheel. Over the last thirteen years all I've done is chase my tail. Yes, I've loved the success, the adulation, the money, the power. But when you're sixty years old you have to ask yourself, What the fuck am I doing it for? I run from one project to another, fighting the clock. Fighting for an hour with my granddaughter, or an hour with my husband or my children. For what? At the end of the day all we have is each other. With any luck, I'll make it to seventy-five. And if I do, what will I have? Hopefully my husband and my kids, and memories. But do I really want to spend the rest of my life running around the world to get my face on TV? I'm not building a career, I'm way past that. Why was it never enough to be a manager, a wife and a mother? I got the taste of fame. I do truly love working in TV. Has it now become my drug? Yes. I've met amazing people, made amazing friends. Done incredible things, but I do realise that you can't have it all. Because of my work schedule and Ozzy's, we've been parted for weeks at a time. Not good. Not healthy.

And it's my fault. For the last thirteen years I've lived a life of no balance; it's been either great highs or deep lows. The truth is, if I was Ozzy I'd be pissed off with me too. In fact, I am pissed off at myself. You'd think that at this age I'd have it all sorted. I'm as clueless now as I was at sixteen. The only difference is that I'm aware of it now. And I'm trying. My catchwords now are 'balance' and 'moderation'. I'll let you know.

16

The Wild Card

Making my *X Factor* return in typically OTT style!

When I accepted Richard Curtis's invitation in 2013 to do a sketch for Comic Relief, it wasn't just altruism at work, nor even the opportunity to work with David Walliams. It was the script. The working title was 'Simon Cowell's Wedding', and Simon himself had agreed to be involved. I hadn't seen him since the last episode of *America's Got Talent*, when I'd walked out. Then there had been the business of his biography, and my telling the world on live TV that he had a small dick. Almost a year had passed since we'd declared our truce over the phone on the day Pearl was born, but saying that you're all fine with each other is one thing; you never know for sure until you see the whites of their eyes.

———

And it wasn't only Simon who would be there. If they all played ball, it would be a roll call of *X Factor* faces. And as I was whisked through the English countryside after landing at Heathrow, I had butterflies in my stomach. Whether it was nerves or excitement, I don't know. More likely a combination of both.

The conceit of the sketch is that Simon is standing at the altar with a mystery bride whose face is obscured by a veil. As this is his wedding, all his various friends and acquaintances are there in the congregation.

When I arrived, Simon was filming some of his scenes, so we just nodded and smiled at each other across the pews. *Britain's Got Talent* judges Amanda Holden and Alesha Dixon were there, dressed as bridesmaids, and the seated guests included previous contestants Stavros Flatley, Rylan Clark, Pudsey the dog and Sinitta, dressed only in palm fronds and weeping because *she* wasn't the bride. Paul Potts led a choir made up of those gorgeous boys from JLS. It was quite a cast.

Meanwhile, in a room at the back of the church, were Dermot O'Leary, Olly Murs, David Walliams and I, all waiting for our big moment.

As Simon was about to take his vows, David ran up

the aisle and tried to stop 'my Simon' from marrying the mystery bride, followed swiftly by Olly Murs, Dermot O'Leary and Louis Walsh all wearing white gowns too and declaring undying love for him. I nearly wet myself when I saw Louis wearing what was supposed to be a replica of Kate Middleton's wedding dress but which, on him, looked as if it had been cobbled together from my nan's curtains.

Then came my entrance as, bursting into the church, also wearing a wedding dress, I push aside these other contenders for Simon's hand.

'Simon, *I* want to marry you.'

'Really?' He looked perplexed. 'But I thought you hated me.'

'I do. But I want to marry you so that I can ruin the rest of your life.'

Needless to say, he turns me down, then lifts the veil of the bride to reveal that he is marrying himself.

As a sketch it was absolutely hilarious, cleverly taking the piss out of all of us. And it was particularly brave of Simon, I thought. Although I was laughing along with the rest of them, it felt weird finding myself in a wedding dress, given the state of my marriage. By now the butterflies had totally gone, but the rumblings of nausea were still gurgling away in my stomach. And I realised that they had nothing to do with what was happening here today, and everything to do with the crap I was dealing with back home.

No one present in the church had the faintest clue what I was going through at the time, not even Louis. As I always do in such situations, I was playing good old fun Sharon, being outrageously camp and cracking jokes like the best of them. Anything but reveal the depressing reality of my life at that time.

It felt nice to have some uncomplicated fun without the burden of having to face up to my problems.

Once the director had declared a wrap on filming, the lovely Sinitta came to find me. Thankfully minus the palm fronds by now.

'Are you coming for dinner?'

She and Simon are very old friends, and I knew that the invitation would include him.

'I haven't been asked,' I smiled, glancing over her shoulder as he walked up behind her.

'Of course you have,' he said, rolling his eyes. 'Come on, you've *got* to come.'

The Wild Card

We ended up at the Arts Club in Mayfair, just me, Louis, Simon and his on-off girlfriend Mezhgan Hussainy and Sinitta and her boyfriend. It was just like old times, and we had a great evening, with banter flying back and forth across the table. We talked a lot about things that had gone on in the past, dredging up old stories from the early *X Factor* days.

It felt so lovely to be there, just laughing and joking and not having to worry about anyone else at the table. If Ozzy, by some miracle, had come out with us, I would have spent the duration being his social lubricant because, first, his damaged hearing means he can't always get what people say in noisy restaurants, and second, they can't always understand what *he's* saying, so I have to act as go-between. It was great to sit there and think only of myself.

Occasionally, one of them would ask me a question about Ozzy, and I would just bat it off with, 'Oh, he's being a wanker, the same as usual,' but none of them knew that I really, *really* meant it.

Eventually the coffee cups were cleared away and we all had to leave. Simon's a very hard person to read at the best of times, but as far as I could tell, he had acted perfectly normally with me, both at the church and in the restaurant, so I left feeling relieved that clearly there was no issue between us. Normal service was resumed.

A few weeks later, he called me. Did I want to be a judge on *X Factor Australia*? he asked. The Aussies knew me well because *The Osbournes* was very successful out there.

My immediate thought was, Why the fuck not? A whole change of scene, good money, and, best of all, considering my disposition towards him at the time, I would be thousands of miles away from my husband, who by this point was having the motherfucker of all mid-life crises somewhere in the Buckinghamshire countryside. Send me the contract – where do I bloody sign?

It was Jack who brought me down to earth. 'Listen, Mum, you can't do this. You will make yourself *ill*,' he warned when I told him with great excitement about the offer.

Admittedly, on paper the schedule did look slightly manic, particularly as I was planning to film three live shows of *The Talk* from Tuesday to Thursday, then pre-record one on the Thursday afternoon before hopping on a seventeen-hour flight to Australia for *The X Factor* at weekends then heading back to LA in time to film *The Talk* again on Tuesday. It was clearly insane, but I buried any misgivings and ploughed on with negotiations.

I didn't consult Ozzy because we weren't speaking back then, just exchanging the occasional text about Sabbath business. Looking back, I'm sure that part of my wanting to do the Australian *X Factor* was yet again to prove to him that I was my own person and didn't need his permission to go.

Kelly was the next to join the queue of doom-mongers. 'Mum, you're fucking mad,' she said. 'You cannot *physically* do this, never mind mentally. You're just not up to it. It'll kill you.'

Deep down, I knew she was right. In the AA pro-gramme they call it 'doing a geographic', when people move away because they think it will help solve their problems. But of course you can never escape what's going on inside your own head. In the end, it was Jack who finally broke through to me.

'If you do this, Mum, you'll never get to see Pearl. And even if you do, you'll be like a zombie. Is that what you want?'

So, just as it got to the wire, I pulled out. Syco were

pretty annoyed with me, and I don't blame them, but I had finally accepted that running off to the other side of the world, away from my kids and grandkid, was not going to solve my problems. The only way to have made it work would have been to move there for three months solid, which I couldn't do as it would have meant giving up *The Talk*, which had become a lifeline for me.

Then, a couple of days later, I got a call from Richard Holloway, executive producer of *The X Factor* UK and the man who had tried so valiantly to act as mediator between me and Dannii Minogue all those years ago. Would I be interested in returning as a judge for the tenth anniversary series, which started filming in three months' time?

'Is this a fucking wind-up?'

'No, darling, absolutely not. It's the real deal.'

I still couldn't quite believe it. During one of our weekly phone calls, Louis and I had discussed the possibility of me going back, but only in a nostalgic, wouldn't-it-be-lovely kind of way. I don't think either of us imagined it would actually happen.

Yet here they were, at Simon's instigation I presumed, offering me a chance to complete the circle, to go back for this milestone series and put things right. I had hated leaving like I did, so I relished the thought of going back to see all the old crew and picking up where I'd left off.

When I told the kids, they *still* thought it was a bad idea because of the major travel involved, but LA to London was far more doable than the flight to Australia. And, from my point of view, as I told them, the opportunity to make amends *and* distract myself from the chaotic state of my marriage was too good to miss. So I said yes, yes, YES!

I hadn't breathed a word about it to Ozzy, who was now away on tour and still attempting to stay sober. I wasn't hiding anything from him, as we weren't living together when the negotiations started, and I didn't think it was any of his fucking business at that time.

The first two days of filming were 4 and 5 June in Glasgow, and I jetted in from LA the night before. I was really looking forward to it, but also felt slightly unnerved by being the new girl on an already established judging panel. Would I fit in?

Obviously, I knew I was replacing former judge Tulisa Contostavlos, and that Louis had really enjoyed working with her, but other than that I didn't really know much about her. However, just before I arrived in Glasgow, a story had broken about her allegedly setting up a drug deal for an undercover reporter, and I felt nothing but sympathy for the poor girl. She's young, she's vulnerable and she doesn't seem to have good people around her. Or she does, and she's not listening to their advice. But either way, everything is celebrity-driven now and you have to know how to handle that, but how can you when you're still in your early twenties? That could so easily have been Kelly when she was hanging out with the wrong crowd in London, so even though I had never met Tulisa, my heart went out to her.

My advice to her would be to stay away from alcohol for a while and perhaps go through some therapy to deal with any issues, then keep a very low profile until it all blows over. I would say, use that time to rethink your life and where you want to be for the next few years, because she has got a lot going for her. She just needs to take stock and look at who she's hanging around with, what their influence is on her. She's only young; she can come back from it.

The Wild Card

Myself and the other judges were all staying at the Grosvenor Hilton in the city and, of course, quite a crowd of fans and assorted media had gathered outside the entrance. As I stepped out of the car, a number of autograph books were pushed in my direction and I started signing them as the fans and journalists shouted questions at me. It was utter chaos.

'Sharon! How does it feel to be back on *X Factor*?'

'I love it.'

'Sharon, what do you think of Glasgow?'

'I love it.'

'Sharon, what do you think of Tulisa . . .'

I couldn't hear the rest of the sentence above the mayhem, so just stuck with the same shtick.

'I love it.'

As soon as the words left my mouth, I realised that answering a question you can't hear is a very stupid thing to do. I should have known that, given my years of experience of having remarks thrown at me on red carpets around the world. But it was too late.

It turned out that they'd asked me what I thought of Tulisa being in trouble. Shit. And, of course, the next day they ran a story about her with my quote tagged on the end as if I was gloating about a young girl having a bad time, which I would never do. So that pissed me off no end. What a great start.

Once inside the hotel, I established that all the other judges had arrived and insisted we all meet in the bar for 'one drink', just to hang out a bit before we started filming the very next morning. Well, one drink led to another. Then another. There was no food, not even a slice of cake, so the booze went straight to our heads. We finally got to bed at 4 a.m., and had to be up three and a half hours later!

Louis and I are old friends, and I know Nicole Scherzinger from way back too. I first met her in LA, when she was still in the Pussycat Dolls, and thought she was just the most *magnificent* young woman. She is one of those women you look at and go, wow. But not only does she have a face and figure that are jaw-dropping, she is beautiful on the inside too and *such* a grafter. My God, she has worked her butt off for every last thing she has in life and she never takes her success for granted. I adore her.

When I did what turned out to be my last *X Factor* in 2007, she had come out to Los Angeles to help me choose my finalists at the judges' house, and I see her around and about occasionally over there too. We have a great relationship, and it's only got better since working on this year's series together.

The only judge I didn't know was Gary Barlow, though I respected him enormously as an artist. There wasn't a Take That tour I hadn't seen, so I hoped that when we finally met we would gel – and we did.

We all clicked immediately, no doubt assisted by the alcohol we consumed that first night, but from then on we just hit a rhythm and it worked. The four of us complement each other well – two artists and two managers looking at things from a different perspective – and we're careful to give each other the space and time to say our piece without talking across each other. And as many of the camera and sound guys were the same ones who had done the 2007 series, it was like putting on a comfy pair of old slippers. It was friendly but, best of all, it was fun.

'I was nice and professional before you joined,' Gary told me after a few days. 'Now you've turned me into a naughty boy.'

It was true. The four of us were back in the hotel bar

in Glasgow, all wearing our dressing gowns, a rule I had insisted upon for comfort, and one that stuck for the duration of filming the audition stages.

Gary's eyes had popped out of his head when I first suggested it, but soon he didn't give a shit. We must have looked a right sight to other guests staying in the hotels on our itinerary across the country, but at the end of each day's filming, we all felt very wired and the surge of adrenalin wasn't something we could just switch off. We needed to unwind, to sit and just be silly for a bit, and the bar was the best place to do that. Also, it felt liberating for us to have conversations together that weren't being bloody filmed.

I corrupted Gary during filming, too. After a few polite responses to contestants on the first day on set, it didn't take me long to hit my stride on the insults, particularly when it was one of those ear-wiltingly bad singers who has auditioned before and just wants to be on TV for a painful few seconds. We could all spot them a mile off, but unlike the others, I couldn't be arsed to be polite about it.

'Fuck off, you're wasting our time,' I told one man who looked like he'd come straight from the pub and didn't even know the proper words to the song he was supposedly trying to impress us with.

I could see that Gary was rather unsettled by my bluntness, but after a succession of piss-poor acts he finally snapped and started talking my language.

'Nah, fuck off, you're rubbish.'

Bad auditions like these were fun in small doses, but if you got a run of them it could be very wearing. Then, every so often, an act would wander in that reminded me why I loved doing the show.

In 2007, when I last did the show, a fourteen-year-old girl called Stephanie Woods auditioned and got through to my judges' house stage in Hollywood, the one where Nicole was helping me. But we didn't put her through to the live finals because she was just so young, and I felt it was too soon for that kind of pressure. She was a genuinely nice girl, but she wasn't as street-smart as the others and I thought, I can't do this to you. It's too much. Afterwards, I wrote her a note telling her that she was a star and shouldn't give up on her dream.

Fast-forward six years, and she turned up with my note in her hand. It was such an incredible moment for me, really humbling. She's twenty now, and working in a normal job, not singing, but she auditioned again and this time got through to the next stage, so we'll see what happens.

The first major difference I noticed between the first four series of *The X Factor* and the current one is how the absence of Simon made it much harder work. When he was on board, he would flatly refuse to start filming before noon, so it meant the rest of us got a lie-in too. Invariably he would turn up a couple of hours late anyway, so it meant we wouldn't get going until 2 p.m. or 3 p.m., but I didn't care because me and Louis would sit around chatting with the production crew, gossiping about what was in the papers and catching up on everyone's lives. It was a job, yes, but it also felt like a little family. Prior to the arrival of Dannii Minogue, I had always actively looked forward to going. It had never felt like work.

This time, however, it did. The judges all got along swimmingly, so that wasn't the issue. It was the interminably long hours, and that there was seemingly no escape from the cameras. The only place we weren't filmed was the toilet, and even then, within two minutes someone would be banging on the door saying I was needed on set. It felt a bit like being on *Big Brother*.

For the audition shows, my alarm would go off at 7.30 a.m. and I would hop in the bath to try and wake myself up. As I rise early each day for *The Talk*, it wasn't the getting up as such that fazed me, it was the jet lag, because I would have just flown in from LA, which is eight hours behind the UK. So my body thought it was getting up at 11.30 p.m.

Meanwhile, my wardrobe supremo Maggie would have quietly let herself into the suite, and be steaming about three outfits for me to choose from for that day's filming. Then there would be a request from someone in production for me to wear something with a 'splash of colour', and I would completely ignore them and wear what I liked, which was usually black or cream.

After my bath, I would emerge from my bedroom to find Maggie steaming away, my make-up artist Trisha ready to beautify me and my assistant Claire ready and waiting with my pot of tea, a few slices of lemon and either a bowl of bran or a couple of poached eggs.

Just like every other woman on television, I like to have my own people around me. All the people who work with me have done so for years. I consider them to be extended family. Trisha knows that when you get to my age, good make-up is all in the blending. If my regular hairdresser Lino isn't around, she does my hair too. Then it's on with that day's chosen outfit and into the car to head to the filming location for 10 a.m. sharp.

In Manchester, we filmed at Old Trafford, a stunningly high-end stadium with fantastic facilities where we could each have had a private room to sit in during downtime. Except that there was very little downtime any more, because just about everything was filmed and we were constantly followed by the cameras.

During the occasional five-minute breaks, the other three judges and I would be taken to a communal room where the make-up artists and production crew sit, and we would be filmed the entire time, even while I was slurping a quick bowl of soup.

When Simon was in situ, he was also acting as producer, which he does superbly. He has a fantastic eye, a natural instinct for knowing what makes great television. Yes, *The X Factor* is a talent show, but it's also a TV show and he would be editing in his head as we went along. Both Louis and I learnt so much from him in the first four series because he would regularly tick us off, explaining that if we had taken this or that road with that contestant, this or that would have happened and then there would have been a great scenario at the end of it, but we didn't . . .

But the new philosophy seems to be film absolutely *everything* and let's see how it pans out. I know that TV shows have to evolve to stay on top, and that they are trying to make the viewer feel more involved by filming everything backstage too, but it's much more draining for the judges because from 10 a.m. to 11 p.m., when filming wrapped, we would rarely get a break from the exposing eye of the camera lens.

Most nights, after a couple of wind-down drinks with the others in the bar, I would get back to my room, exhausted, then start making telephone calls, first to the kids to make sure they were OK, then to Julie in LA to go through any Black Sabbath business or other work matters. So to say I felt shattered the next day would be a masterly understatement, but it would be the same relentless schedule again until that phase of filming finished and I would hop back on a plane to LA.

I wasn't complaining; they were paying me well and I wanted to do it. But there were plenty of times when I was reminded that I'm not getting any younger. I was also missing my family terribly, and when Jack or Lisa put Pearl on Facetime to me, I would have a little sob afterwards.

So now it's the first live audition show of the tenth anniversary season and Louis, Gary, Nicole and I are standing at the back of Wembley Arena, tucked out of sight of the crowd. It's a vast space, but the collective heat of the assembled bodies on this hot July day is overpowering, though thankfully it does nothing to diminish the buzz of excitement.

The usual handful of production staff with clipboards and earpieces hovers around. One of them, a young girl, smiles warily at me, presumably because my reputation for speaking my mind precedes me. I smile back and give her a little wink, just to reassure her that I don't bite.

Simon's long-standing warm-up man, Ian Royce, is going through his routine, making them howl with laughter and whipping them up into the high-octane frenzy you need to create an atmosphere on TV – otherwise the filter of the camera lens kills it stone dead.

I close my eyes for a couple of seconds, trying to control the butterflies in my stomach. Perhaps sensing my unease, Louis throws an arm around my shoulder and gives it a little squeeze.

'You OK?'

I simply nod and smile, focusing in on the fact that Roycie is in the throes of finishing his routine.

I want to do this. I need to do it, for closure. To put things right.

Apart from the long hours, the audition stages of the past few weeks have been water off a duck's back, particularly as we returned to the old format of doing them in a small room with just the four of us and the contestant present. But you're operating in a vacuum because the shows don't get aired until several months later, so you have no idea how you're coming across or being received.

Today is different. We are at Wembley Arena and, for the first time since rejoining, I will walk out in front of a live studio audience. My insides are on fucking spin cycle.

A live studio audience is that deeply scary unknown factor, the reaction of which you can never take for granted. They will either love you, in which case they'll raise the rafters, or they'll hate you and boo with all the gusto of a pantomime audience when the wicked witch appears on stage. And there isn't a damn thing I can do to predict or change which of those two reactions it's going to be.

I'd like to be able to say that I couldn't give a damn whether they liked me or not, but it's not true. I do. And even if ninety-eight per cent of that audience is cheering, I will only hear the two per cent who are expressing their dislike of me.

'Ladies and gentlemen, let's hear it for the *X Factor* judges!' booms Roycie. It's time.

As the four of us walk down the central aisle through the 4,000-strong crowd, they go absolutely wild, cheering, whistling, clapping and even stamping their feet. I feel the vibrations through the floor as I walk towards the raised judges' table in front of the stage.

This is the part I love. The moment when the performance begins and I surf the wave of audience reaction, feeling like the Queen of the World lifted up with their applause. It's a mini version of what rock stars feel when they walk out on stage and thousands of people simultaneously roar their approval. The adrenalin surge it gives you is the most amazing feeling and is, therefore, addictive.

That's why the Rolling Stones are still putting on shows when most men their age are tending an allotment somewhere. It's not about the money; it's about that adrenalin high, about public approval.

Nicole grins at me and I can see that she's enjoying the buzz too, but to my mind the cheer has been for her and the others, the returning favourites, not for me. As far as I'm concerned, the audience reaction to my return has yet to be determined.

I smile broadly and wave at no one in particular, not daring to focus on any one person in case I see an expression that unsettles me. Then Gary takes the microphone.

'Hello, Wembley!'

They cheer even louder. The crowd's affection for him is palpable across the venue.

'Guess who's back?'

Suddenly, I'm aware of my name being chanted in

unison, starting low, building up steam, then swelling to a loud crescendo, a Mexican wave of sound.

Sha-ron! Sha-ron! Sha-ron!

At last, I dare to focus on individual faces, and the warmth they exude is overwhelming. I can feel tears of relief pricking my eyes and blink rapidly to force them back. Whatever they have read, or thought, about me in the past, good or bad, it is clearly forgotten now and their acceptance of me is universal, their welcome truly humbling. Suddenly, the rumblings in my stomach disappear and I beam up at them, waving my arm with a queenly flourish before tilting my head and bowing in thanks at their graciousness. Gary hands me the mike.

'It's so good to be back,' I shout as they start clapping again. 'And thank you so much for giving me such a great welcome. It means a lot.'

I take my seat at the judges' table and a warm feeling of something approaching happiness envelops me.

It was well past midnight by the time we were through the final day of boot camp. Late as it was, the adrenalin was still pumping and we all went back to Gary's hotel and retreated to the bar, as had become our practice, though this time we were not in our dressing gowns. We were drained, all four of us, and began talking about what we were going to do next year when the show finished. Gary planned to go back on tour, and work on a new album. Because that's what he does. That's his day job. It was the same for Nicole; she was going back into the studio and then on tour. They were both leaving to get back to their lives. Louis too had decided it was time to bow out and is already planning his new boy band.

As for me, Simon gave me the opportunity to return, and I will always be grateful to him for that. But I won't be doing it next year; physically I just can't. *This* was my year, my last hurrah, my chance to complete the circle and put a few old ghosts to rest. I had something to prove. I wanted it to be the perfect finale – ten years of something I had been a part of starting.

There has been much discussion over the last few years about the rights and wrongs of talent shows such as ours, and the effect they have had on the music industry. Many accomplished artists think their impact is all negative. In some ways I agree with them. It has altered the psyche of young people. A generation of kids has grown up thinking it's easy to become a star. But many of the contestants have gone on to earn their living in the industry, and without the show it would never have happened. Many of them have become true stars. The real prize is to be able to work at something you love. The acid test is the same as it's always been: those with true talent will last, and the instant-coffee people will not.

But as Louis, Gary, Nicole and I agreed in the bar, whether we are there or not, *The X Factor* will go on without us, giving hope and entertainment and allowing real talent to emerge. And the thing that we will take away with us is our friendship.

It was gone 5 a.m. by the time we left. We all had flights booked – Gary to LA, Nicole to Europe, Louis back to Ireland and me to Heathrow. I had a 7 a.m. flight to New York to catch, to join my husband and the band at their base for a few days as they played Toronto, Chicago and Indianapolis.

As for me, I have new responsibilities and new priorities.

Pearly girl, here's my Christmas gift to you: Nana's coming home to stay.

Epilogue

'Fucking hell, Sharon, we've had twenty-seven houses in thirty fucking years! *Please* tell me we don't have to move again . . .'

Ozzy is standing in the driveway of our new, rented house on North Crescent Drive, the one I spent so many happy times in with Gert and Sonny, and he's staring open-mouthed at the number of packing boxes scattered around the place.

'Stop fretting, Dadda.' I pull him towards me and kiss his forehead. 'Why don't you go and make us a cup of tea?'

He shuffles off towards the kitchen and I stand on the steps at the front of the house, drinking in the beauty of the crescent-shaped garden in front of me. Bella, my

Pomeranian, is in my arms, my living, breathing stress ball. Caressing her soft ears always soothes me, and I do so now as I contemplate what my husband has just said.

It's true. We have moved a ridiculous number of times in my pursuit of the 'perfect' home, the one that's going to be our 'for ever' house. But then I start picking fault. It's too far away, it's too close to the road, it's too big, it's too small. And then we're off again, packing our life into boxes and hitting the road.

I realise now that the houses have had nothing to do with it; thinking that if the garden were just a tiny bit bigger, or the location just a little more convenient, *then* our marriage would be happy ever after. But of course, mine and Ozzy's addictions, and the emotional peaks and troughs they bring, can't be left behind. They're in a box that always comes with us, resting in some dark recess of the new place until, once again, it's opened and they cause trouble.

Rocky appears in the doorway, blinking against the piercing midday sunshine, and I know that Ozzy isn't far behind. Rocky is Ozzy's dog, as Bella is mine. They follow us everywhere with blind, unconditional devotion. If only humans could be that uncomplicated.

Epilogue

Ozzy reappears as predicted and hands me a cup of tea. We stand in silence together for a little while, enjoying this brief moment of peace. It's Sunday and the house is quiet, just me, Ozzy and the dogs pottering around the place. Jack is away filming so, just before lunch, Lisa will bring Pearl over for a few hours. We'll eat, and then Lisa will slip off to the spare room for some much-needed sleep while the devoted grandparents keep watch.

Ozzy is so besotted with Pearl that he can't take his eyes off her. When she was here the other day, he scooped her up in his arms, her alabaster skin so pale against the dark spread of his tattoos, and went all Jane Austen on us, taking her for 'a turn around the garden'.

'Look, Pearl, this is Nana's rose garden,' he said, pulling off a fresh white petal and handing it to her. 'And *this* is where we grow vegetables.'

Yes, you read that right. The once rabble-rousing Osbournes have an allotment.

Wherever Pearl is, Kelly is never far away. She *adores* her niece and plays the flamboyant, irreverent, slightly batty aunt to perfection. I just know that, despite the age difference, she will be a fantastic friend to Pearl when she grows up, and no doubt her own children will form a bond with their cousin too.

Later, I will make us all lunch – correction: *order* lunch from the Beverly Hills Hotel (some things will never change), and we'll sit around the kitchen table and chat away, all focusing on darling Pearl and her hearty appetite, laughing as one of the dogs rushes in for a dropped titbit and spits out the slice of courgette in disgust.

Right now, the table is covered in the white plastic crates that are full of Ozzy's oils and pencils. He sat there and drew for an hour this morning, the light streaming in through the window. He likes to lose himself in it, but it can be tricky for him to concentrate when he's sitting in the hub of the house.

I take his hand and lead him up a set of stairs at the side of the garage. This is the only two-storey part of the house. We squeeze past at least twenty removal boxes with 'Ozzy's Books' scribbled on the side, and walk into the large room above the garage. It is wood-panelled, with parquet flooring, a vast antique desk and three black leather sofas scattered around it, one placed right in front of a fifty-inch plasma TV screen.

Epilogue

This will be Ozzy's man cave. It is the second room I have started work on, after Pearl's nursery. Yes, I'm still bloody mothering him in so many ways, but I know that this room – Ozzy having his own space – will make him happy.

We all need a place to escape to in our lives, don't we? In every house we've occupied, Ozzy has always had a bunker, as we call it. I will bring his paints up here, line the shelves with his treasured history books and music awards and hang his favourite photos and paintings on the walls. Already I have slung his two rubber bats over the chandelier to make him feel at home.

Just after Ozzy and I reconciled, something momentous happened in our marriage. It was the Daytime Emmy Awards, and *The Talk* was up for five awards, including best talk show. All my co-hosts were going with their husbands or partners, there to support the achievement of their loved ones. In the past, getting Ozzy to a high-profile event like this was like pulling fucking teeth. He would never want to come to the Brits; when we won an Emmy for *The Osbournes* he didn't come; the Grammys, the National Television Awards . . . the list of functions Ozzy has shunned is

---

endless. The only one he likes is the Pride of Britain Awards because he loves the stories of courage. But other than that, he would either cause an argument so he didn't have to attend, or come along and, while being all sweetness and light to everyone else, would be muttering in my ear about me being 'Mrs Fucking TV'. I understood it, because he hated all the bullshit that went with it, but at the same time it meant that I felt unsupported.

So when I asked him to escort me to the Daytime Emmys, I wasn't holding out much hope. But he said yes, just like that, without fuss, recrimination or sarcasm. And he was immensely supportive to me there, affectionate too. It meant the world to me, and I honestly couldn't believe it was happening. For the first time in our marriage, I felt that he had finally accepted that I have a life outside him, and that he no longer feels threatened by it.

He still moans when I go away to do *X Factor*, but now his tone is wistful rather than condemning. I simply point out to him that when I'm in LA, we have a lot more time together than people who hold down a nine-to-five job.

'This room should all be finished by the end of next

week,' I say, studying the large photograph of him and Kelly that he loves so much, already hanging to one side of the TV. I know he'll feel more settled then.

I leave him there, sorting through his books and knick-knacks, and walk back down the stairs, back past the allotment and into the main house. The large black-and-white marble hallway is wonderfully cool in the heat of the day.

The spare bedroom is my unofficial wardrobe, at the moment. Racks and racks of clothes line the walls, a testament to my shopping addiction. About seventy per cent of it is black, about twenty-five per cent cream or white, with just a small splash of colour here and there. My possessions used to be my crutch, my comfort blanket. But now I feel weighed down by them. The plan is to sort through it all and have a clothing sale, perhaps at Christmas, to raise money for my colon cancer programme. That way, I won't feel so guilty about the money I have wasted on my fashion gluttony. I'm like one of those men who chase a woman, then lose interest as soon as they get her. Except my weakness doesn't hurt anyone's feelings, though Ozzy may beg to differ.

I pad through our bedroom to the huge en suite that Ozzy reckons is about the same size as the entire downstairs floor of the terraced house he grew up in. At one end of it is a door leading out to our private patio, where the sun is reflecting off the water in our cute *à deux* hot tub. Have we ever been in it? Have we fuck. Nice to have it though, eh? And the birds like to wash themselves in it.

I walk round the side of the house to the swimming pool, where I find Ozzy doing a sedate breaststroke.

'It's so fucking hot, I had to cool down.'

The temperature is nudging ninety degrees now, and when you dress in as much black as Ozzy does, it probably feels like twice that.

'Why don't you get dry, Dadda, and we'll go to the hotel coffee shop for an iced drink?'

Sure, I could make him an iced drink here, but my new mission is to get Ozzy out of the house as much as I can. It helps that the kids don't live with us any more, because every so often we hop in the car and visit them, something he *never* complains about.

And last week it was our thirty-first wedding anniversary. I flew to LA from filming the *X Factor* auditions in Cardiff, Ozzy met me at the airport and we drove to Laguna Beach for the weekend with Rocky and Bella. It was glorious. We just walked along the beach, had massages and hung out together, enjoying each other's company. And he bought me a beautiful gold and diamond necklace.

What a contrast to *last* year, and that seemingly interminable day of hell in a New York hotel room. It's amazing how, in just one year, our marriage has gone from that to this. At the time, I would never have believed it possible.

We talked about it a little bit, but he doesn't remember much because he was so out of his mind at the time. He never brings the subject up, but when I do, he no longer bats me away, and he accepts that his behaviour was reprehensible. *That's* a breakthrough, too.

I hand him a towel and head back into the house to find my handbag while he dries himself off.

The beauty, and the price, of this new house is that it's just one block away from the world-famous Beverly Hills Hotel, an iconic pink and green building that has played host to countless A-list celebrities over the years. One of its regulars was the famously reclusive Howard

_____

Hughes, who would have staff leave him roast-beef sandwiches in the crook of the tree outside his secluded bungalow room in the grounds so he didn't have to talk to anyone. I reckon my husband would do that if I let him.

Five minutes later, me and Ozzy buzz ourselves out of the electric side gate and on to a deserted North Crescent Drive. This is an area that oozes wealth and, consequently, all the houses are of South Fork dimensions – except for ours – and no one walks anywhere.

Oh, hang on, did I say the road was deserted? Correction: here comes another bloody tour bus, with some numpty on a Tannoy wittering on about who lives where. Except that most of them have moved out long ago, and the mugs in the bus are none the wiser.

We were driven out of our home on Doheny Drive by them. Our fault, I know, because it was the house we filmed *The Osbournes* in. But it was quite close to the road and we suffered interminable Tannoy noise all day long, from early morning until late at night. There are no restrictions on them in LA, so they can do the hours they want.

_____

Epilogue

We sold the house to Christina Aguilera, who stayed there for seven years, presumably with earplugs in, and she's now sold it to someone else and moved further out.

We set off down the hill and Ozzy, who is carrying my bright orange tote for me, spots the tour bus and literally throws the bloody thing at me.

'I'm the Prince of Fucking Darkness. I can't be seen carrying a fucking handbag.'

As the open-topped minibus approaches, I can hear the tour guide saying something about Gloria Swanson and Milton Berle, who both lived near here when Moses was a boy, then watch with amusement as one of the occupants clocks Ozzy and starts pointing and shrieking. They can't believe they are seeing an actual living, breathing celebrity.

Suddenly, they're all crushed to one side of the bus, snapping away as Ozzy picks up a walking speed I didn't know he possessed and disappears over a small hedge that borders the grounds of the Beverly Hills Hotel.

On our return, we are greeted with: 'Mum, where the fuck have you been?'

It's my darling, searingly direct daughter Kelly who has arrived with fiancé Matthew for lunch to find no one home. She's standing in front of the wine rack in the kitchen, stocked solely with small bottles of Evian, hands on hips and glaring at me.

'Me and Dadda went to the coffee shop and got lunch.' I hold up one of two Beverly Hills Hotel distinctive striped carrier bags, stuffed to the top with salads, club sandwiches, fries and various sauces. I see her indignation deflate slightly.

The buzzer for the main gate sounds. Lisa has arrived with the precious cargo we've all gathered to see: the delicious Pearl. She's such a genial child, so chilled yet so enquiring. Ozzy marvels at how quickly she learns things and, just like every other devoted granddad, tells anyone who'll listen how intelligent she is. She even managed to switch on the television the other day, which impressed him no end.

'Pearly girl!' I lift her into the air and kiss the end of her cute button nose, pulling her into my side, her nappy-clad bottom resting on my hip.

We wander inside. Kelly and Matthew clear the kitchen table of Ozzy's paints and drawing pads, while

Epilogue

Lisa straps Pearl into her highchair and I tip all the salads and sauces into various bowls.

Placing the cutlery on the table, I sit down next to Lisa who is chopping up bits of carrot, tomato and broccoli for Pearl, who is wolfing it down. They are all chatting animatedly about something they have seen on the celebrity website TMZ that morning, and I take the opportunity just to sit back, study them all and let my mind flow with rare, uninterrupted thoughts. Whenever I do this, I always think of all the things I should have done but didn't. Perhaps now it's time to make sure I don't do the same in the future.

You forget so much of your life and the road you've taken to get to where you are, but now I'm sixty, I find myself reflecting more. I think about the milestone events, the people who have drifted in and out of my life, the people I've lost to illness and the good friends I have gained.

And the battles. Oh my God, *always* fighting with someone about something. People used to write things about my husband, or my kids, and I would go *insane*. When you're younger, you think you can fight the world, but now I know you can't. There's good and there's bad in life, and there's not a damned thing you can do to change that. Even to try is so draining. But if you say anything nasty about my husband or my kids to my face, I'll probably still belt you.

When my father died, all the fights he'd had, the business deals he'd got himself in such states about, the fancy cars and houses he owned depending on whether he was bankrupt that week or not . . . at the end, his life boiled down to that room in the Belmont rest home in LA. Everything else was history. Besides, the cruelty of Alzheimer's had robbed him of his past anyway. He couldn't remember any of it. At the end of your days, it's all about who cares enough to be standing there when you take your last breath. It's all about family.

And yes, my family is complex, dramatic, irreverent, unorthodox . . . but God, I love them.

All my life I have been pursuing *something*. Be it the next business deal, the next house or the next miracle beauty treatment for eternal youth. But now, the chase is over and I am finally starting to feel something close to contentment. That doesn't mean my life is perfect, far from it. It simply means that I have grown to accept

Epilogue

the flaws I can't change, and do something about the ones I can.

'Do you know what, Sharon?' Ozzy said to me the other day. 'It feels like we're on the last ten minutes of our lives.'

He's right. And I'm going to slow down, sit back and make the most of every last second of it.

Biblidography

Bella

Bella is top dog after the death of Minnie, and goes absolutely everywhere with me. She is registered as a service dog because of all the illnesses I've had, so she can sit on my lap on a commercial flight. She is an apricot-coloured Pomeranian and she is three years old. I bought her from a breeder in North Carolina and Kelly flew to get her.

When her hair is cut short, she looks like a very cute Disney pussy cat. Some people say she looks like Boo, the famous Pomeranian they call 'the cutest dog in the world' and who has her own Facebook page. Bella has a bizarre habit of running and hiding when someone she doesn't know comes *into* the room, then barking hysterically when they leave. She might be tiny and girly, with her pink sparkly collar, but she snores like a trooper. It drives Ozzy mad because she sleeps at the bottom of our bed each night.

Rocky aka Rock Star

Rocky is Ozzy's dog and he wears an Ozzfest bandanna round his neck to confirm the fact. When Ozzy is home,

Rocky is never far from his side. He's also three years old and came from the same breeder as Bella, but from a different litter. He is black and brown with long hair and is the worst guard dog in the world. Anyone could walk into the house and he just wouldn't care. He also sleeps with us, but lies on our heads. He likes to eat my hair.

Bunny

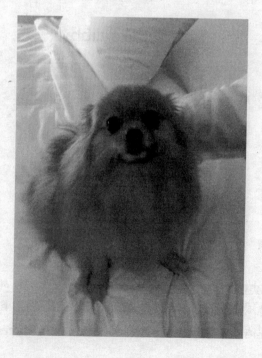

A ginger Pomeranian who is four years old. I got her from a breeder in Miami. We were on holiday there when I saw an advert in the local paper, and that was it. She's neurotic and quite hyper, so she's all over you like a rash and always moving around. She sometimes sleeps with us, but it gets a bit noisy in there because Bella and Rocky bark at her every time she moves, which is most of the time. So Ozzy invariably ends up kicking her out.

Liberty, aka Libby

I bought her at a pet store in New York last summer (2012). She was my comfort buy after the horrible *America's Got Talent* experience. She's part Maltese, part

Shih Tzu, and is gorgeously white and fluffy. I don't usually buy from pet stores any more, because all the dogs I have bought in one tend to have health problems and cost you a fortune in vet bills. But in a way I felt like I was liberating her. She's a very submissive, low-key dog who just likes to be cuddled. She also comes into bed sometimes. The top dogs bark at her, but she doesn't fight back, she just disappears under the covers.

Puff

Another Pomeranian, she's white with apricot-coloured ears. She's four years old and she's a rescue dog that Aimee found online. She is very timid. She just licks you all the time, seeking reassurance and love. Which, of course, in this dog-mad house of ours, she gets in abundance.

Storm

A white husky we rescued from Aspen seven years ago. She was about seven when we got her, so she's quite an old lady now. A friend of mine was on holiday skiing and called to say she had seen this sleigh dog that was about to be put down because her back legs had gone. She wanted to know if I would have her, and of course I said yes. Her legs are really bad now, so she can't walk for long and sleeps a lot. But she still has so much love to give and she's a gorgeous, serene dog. She has a disconcerting habit of making this haunting howling noise, but it's not pain, it's like a call to the wild.

Two Face

She's seven years old and is meant to be a Pomeranian but I reckon there's a bit of something else in there too. I got her from a rescue centre after an Amish puppy farm just outside Philadelphia had been raided. Boy, can she run and jump, so I suspect she might be part Australian shepherd, too.

Charlie

He's a Yorkshire terrier and is three years old. We bought him at an auction for Holly Robinson Peete's charity. She had got him from a rescue home when he was a puppy. He is such a character. He's like the Artful Dodger from *Oliver*, and I rather think he would suit a jaunty little cap. I might buy him one for Christmas. He's into everything, always jumping up and running around with his tongue hanging out. He has bonded with Two Face, and they do everything as a team.

Crazy Baby

The old lady of the family. She's sixteen years old now and is blind and deaf. She's a Japanese Chin and we bought her at a pet store in the Beverly Center, which has now closed down. Her character is very much like a cat, a little bit neurotic and superior. All the other dogs are always giving her such shit, but she doesn't seem to bother. She gets the prefix because she used to come into a room and go crazy over nothing, like a cat that has seen a ghost.

RIP

Lola

Lola was a bulldog and such a huge part of *The Osbournes*. She was *very* famous, and you could even buy a doll of her. She was Jack's dog and, when she died, I asked him if he thought he could ever replace her. He said he didn't need to because he has his daughter, Pearl, and that he could never love a dog the way he loves her. Lola was thirteen when she died, which, for the breed, is almost a world record. Usually it's ten years and you're done.

Minnie

Died July 2008. As explained in Chapter 2, she was my absolute darling and my best friend. Say no more.

Maggie

Died 2013. A Japanese Chin like Crazy Baby, she was seventeen when she died. We got her at the Beverly Center pet store and she had many health problems but, against the odds, managed to reach old age. Her ashes are in a pot on the living-room fireplace, next to Minnie's.

Picture Credits

Integrated images

Chapter 13   © Brian Aris

Chapter 14   REX/Zelig Shaul

Chapter 15   WIREIMAGE

Chapter 16   REX/ Ross McDairmant Photography

Biblidography

All images from author's personal collection, except Lola – © Jack Osbourne/Twitter (@jackosbourne)

Plate Sections

Section 1

Page 1 Getty Images

Page 2 Top: REX/Ken McKay

Bottom: REX/Ken McKay

Page 3 Top: Author's personal collection

Bottom left: Author's personal collection

Bottom right: © *The Talk*/Instagram (thetalk_cbs)

Page 4 Top: Getty Images

Bottom: Getty Images

Page 5 Top: ABC via Getty Images

Bottom: ABC via Getty Images

———

Picture Credits

Page 6 Top: ABC via Getty Images

Bottom: Getty Images for VH1

Page 7 Top: © Ross Halfin

Bottom: © Ross Halfin

Page 8 Top: Getty Images

Bottom: Getty Images

Section 2

Page 1 Top: TalkbackTHAMES/Rex Features

Middle: NBC via Getty Images

Bottom: NBC via Getty Images

Page 2 Top: WIREIMAGE

Middle: Getty Images

Bottom: Getty Images

Page 3 Top: CBS via Getty Images

Bottom: CBS via Getty Images

Page 4 CBS via Getty Images

Page 5 Top: Mirrorpix

Bottom: © Jack Osbourne/Twitter
(@jackosbourne)

Page 6 Top: Neil Preston/Corbis

Bottom: © Brian Aris

Page 7 Top: © Brian Aris
        Bottom: © Brian Aris
Page 8 Top: © Mark Weiss
        Bottom : © Mark Weiss

Section 3

Page 1 © Brian Aris
Page 2 Clockwise from top left: Kelly, Jack and
        Pearl – © Kelly Osbourne/Instagram (kellyos-
        bourne); Ozzy and Pearl – © Lisa Osbourne/
        www.raddestmom.com; Lisa and Sharon –
        Everett Collection/Rex Features; Sharon and
        Pearl – © Lisa Osbourne/www.raddestmom.
        com; Sharon and Pearl (centre) – © Lisa
        Osbourne/Instagram (mrslisao)
Page 3 Top: Getty Images Entertainment
        Bottom: Getty Images Entertainment
Page 4 Top: Time & Life Pictures/Getty Images
        Middle: Getty Images
        Bottom: The Sun News Syndication
Page 5 Top: Splash/Corbis
        Bottom: WIREIMAGE
Page 6 Top: Ray Burmiston

Picture Credits

Bottom left: FilmMagic

Bottom right: David Fisher/Rex Features

Page 7 Top: Brian J Ritchie/Thames/Rex Features

Bottom: FilmMagic

Page 8 Getty Images

sphere

To buy any of our books and to find out
more about Sphere and Little, Brown Book Group,
our authors and titles, as well as events and
book clubs, visit our website

www.littlebrown.co.uk

and follow us on Twitter

@LittleBrownUK

To order any Sphere titles p & p free in the UK,
please contact our mail order supplier on:

+ 44 (0)1832 737525

Customers not based in the UK should contact
the same number for appropriate postage
and packing costs.